Brad Wright has done it again! Numbers show that doomsayers have got it wrong. Reading *Upside* is the ideal vacation—you feel refreshed and you want to tell everyone about it.

Scot McKnight
*Karl A. Olsson Professor
in Religious Studies
North Park University*

Upside can help correct that glass-is-half-empty-and-probably-leaking pessimism that many of us use when thinking about the world and its problems. Bradley Wright brings broad knowledge and a sense of humor to helping readers understand what's gotten better—and what still needs work.

Joel Best
*Professor of Sociology,
University of Delaware
and bestselling author*

UPSIDE

Bradley R.E. Wright, PhD

SIDE

BETHANY HOUSE PUBLISHERS

a division of Baker Publishing Group
Minneapolis, Minnesota

Published by Bethany House Publishers
11400 Hampshire Avenue South
Bloomington, Minnesota 55438
www.bethanyhouse.com

Bethany House Publishers is a division of
Baker Publishing Group, Grand Rapids, Michigan

Printed in the United States of America

Library of Congress Cataloging-in-Publication Data
Wright, Bradley R. Entner.
        Upside : surprising good news about the state of our world / Bradley R. E. Wright.
        p.   cm.
        Includes bibliographical references.
        Summary: "A research sociologist uses statistics to reveal the state of the world in terms of health, education, violence, etc., showing that in many ways we are in much better shape than the secular and Christian media claims"—Provided by publisher.
        ISBN 978-0-7642-0836-2 (pbk. : alk. paper)
        1. Social history. I. Title.
HN18.3.W75 2011
306.09—dc22   2011008310

Cover design by Lookout Design, Inc.

11   12   13   14   15   16   17   7   6   5   4   3   2   1

To Joshua and Gabriel,
who make my world so much better

CONTENTS

FOREWORD

The good news about bad news is that there is not nearly as much of it as you might think.

The bad news about good news is that good news doesn't tend to sell. Everybody wants to get good news from the doctor and their boss and their (choose one) therapist/stockbroker/fantasy football league commissioner. But it turns out that articles indicating that the economy is running along okay or that rivers are relatively clean don't tend to sell newspapers, which means they don't tend to get written.

People go to conferences that warn about dire situations.

People buy books that say the world is falling apart.

Bad news has probably always had a fascination pull. Paul Revere didn't get famous by riding around saying, "The British stayed home! Go ahead and sleep in tomorrow!"

But living in the Information Age (or perhaps more accurately the Anxious Information Age), we seem to get bad news more often, on more channels, in high-def.

For a variety of reasons, the evangelical Christian community often seems to have a particularly sharp appetite for bad news. Authors and speakers who can document that the younger generation is about to lose their faith, or that churches are about to lose their congregations, or that the nation is about to lose its soul, never seem to run short of listeners, no matter how shaky their case may be.

The gravitational pull of bad news is a problem. Like the little boy who cried wolf, the purveyors of doom can eventually lose all credibility, so when bad news really *does* happen, no one is listening anymore.

But there is good news.

Bradley Wright has written a terrific book.

The good news about this book is that it is not based on optimism; it's based on reality. It turns out that much of the reported bad news is often based on bad data. Ninety percent of all statistics in the media are both negative and inaccurate. (I just made that up. But I'll bet there's a bias in that direction.)

Brad is an academician, a bona fide believer, and a highly engaging writer. He has a passion for people to think well, treat statistics with discernment, and not be chronically alarmist.

He wants to help us quit mistaking negativity with thoughtfulness.

He wants to help us stop mindlessly passing on pessimistic diagnoses that are neither helpful nor accurate.

He wants us to actually be aware of and celebrate good news that is spreading on multiple fronts:

- Crime is getting better (but we think it's getting worse).
- We are working less and playing more (but we think we're playing less and working more).
- Poverty is going down.

Two thousand years ago, a book whose core was *euaggelion*—good news—began to be widely read. We of all people should be able to recognize and celebrate and express gratitude wherever we find it. For all good news is God's good news, and to ignore it, hide it, minimize it, or distort it is neither mentally healthy nor spiritually sound.

So take a deep breath, turn the page, and get ready to be happy.

—John Ortberg, author and pastor of
Menlo Park Presbyterian Church

ACKNOWLEDGMENTS

There's nothing like writing a book to make you realize how much you depend on other people. The original idea for this book came from my editor, Andy McGuire, of Bethany House. I had dabbled with the ideas in chapters 1 and 2 and some of the data in later chapters, but it was Andy's idea to put it all together as a book with the guiding question "Is the world getting better?" Thank you, Andy. I have enjoyed writing this book and, once again, working with you. So, reader, if you like this book, Andy gets credit. (And if you don't, well, just remember whose idea it was.)

My wife and I attend a weekly Bible study, and the people in it have unwaveringly encouraged me and advised me. (Several of them are authors as well.) In fact, we even spent the better part of one Friday evening discussing which topics should be covered in this book. Thank you Amy, Brandon, Chris, Clare, Emma, Ishmael, Jeff, Jen, Jen, Judy, Julie, Kyele, Larissa, Tilly, Todd, and Zara.

Many friends and acquaintances have offered personal support and technical expertise in the process of writing this book. I appreciate you greatly. They include Joel Best, Kyndria Brown, Susan Carozza and her family, Ed Cyzewski, Kevin Deisher, Mark Edwards, Jon Entner, Marc Fey, Jillian Gaither Gregory, Vince Gierer, Scot McKnight, Clarence Mjork, Caragh O'Brien, Phil Secker, the Soroka Family, Joann Tackman, David Weakliem, Freeman Wright, and John

Wright. I also thank the therapists at Crossroads Physical Therapy, especially Chery and Rebecca, who have done me much good.

I thank my agent, Chip MacGregor, for his ongoing encouragement and professional socialization into the world of book writing.

Most of all, I thank my wife, Cathryn, and our sons, Gabriel and Joshua, who add so much joy and richness to my life.

CHAPTER 1

PESSIMISM ABOUT OUR NATION AND WORLD

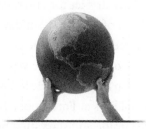

The trouble with this country is that there are too many people going about saying "the trouble with this country is. . . ."
—Sinclair Lewis

If its individual citizens, to a man, are to be believed, [America] always is depressed, and always is stagnated, and always is at an alarming crisis, and never was otherwise.
—Charles Dickens

In an airport bookshop recently, I paused at the current affairs section and looked down the shelves. . . . All [the books] argued to a greater or lesser extent that a) the world is a terrible place and b) it's getting worse. . . . I didn't see a single optimistic book.
—Matt Ridley, science writer

The majority of Americans think that most things in our country and around the world are on a downward spiral, but is such pessimism justified? Is the world really facing impending doom? This book examines data on wide-ranging topics all in service of answering whether things are actually getting better or worse. Think of it as a guided field trip through things that matter. As you read it, you'll find that contrary to popular opinion, life is improving in many ways (though certainly not all), and this improvement is nothing short of remarkable. But before we get into the actual state of the world, let's first look at what we *think* about the state of the world.

Last Thanksgiving I took my nine-year-old son, Floyd,[1] to visit family in the Midwest. Since we were there on a Sunday, we went to a service at the local mega-church, which we had attended and enjoyed before. (They have dry-ice fog and rock guitar during worship—big pluses for both of us.) That Sunday, in the midst of his sermon, the pastor started describing the condition of the world. He began with a story from the local newspaper of an unwanted baby being thrown away in a trash can. He followed this with a story of a mass shooting of soldiers at Fort Hood, Texas. From there he went on to worldwide famine and starvation before finishing with child sex-trafficking. With each malady that he described, he would hang his head and softly cry, "What has this world become?" After about a minute of this litany of suffering, I actually put my hand over Floyd's ears and just smiled at him while he gave me one of his frequent, "Dad, what in the world are you doing?" looks. I'm happy to talk with him about a lot of things, but child sex-trafficking and abandoned babies were not on the docket for that day.

I tell you this story not to criticize the pastor for being unduly negative. I realize that he was just trying to help the audience appreciate the need for the truths he was teaching. But his message illustrates what we routinely hear from so many different sources: that life is bad and getting worse. We know where we're going, and we'll arrive there in a hand basket.

Now, this story is just that—a story—and we can find anecdotal evidence to support just about any position, no matter how farfetched.

So let's consider some systematically collected data to see how widespread our pessimism really is.

The Common Perception of Life Getting Worse

A 2009 nationwide poll asked Americans the following question: "I'd like you to compare the way things are going in the United States to the way they were going five years ago. Generally, would you say things are going better today, worse today, or about the same today as they were going five years ago?" Do you want to guess how many of the respondents thought things are getting worse?[2] A full 83%! Only 5% thought that things were better. That's right: For every one American who thinks that things are getting better, sixteen think they are getting worse.[3]

Another survey question makes the same point. Since 1971, surveys have asked Americans, "Do you feel things in this country are generally going in the right direction, or do you feel things have pretty seriously gotten off on the wrong track?"[4] Now, I like to draw pictures of data, so I have summarized the results of these surveys in Figure 1.1. When this question was asked in 2010, 66% of respondents viewed the country as on the wrong track; only 34% thought we were headed in the right direction. This pessimism is rather typical, for as you can see in Figure 1.1, over most of the last forty years, a majority of Americans have viewed our country as on the wrong track in most years. In only nine years did more respondents say America was headed in the right direction. Overall, about two Americans think that we're on the wrong track for every one who thinks we're going in the right direction. Just a thought, but if we've been on the wrong track for forty years, shouldn't we have arrived in a really bad place already?

Americans aren't just down about our nation as a whole; we're concerned with just about every aspect of it. A 1996 survey asked respondents if they thought the United States was declining or

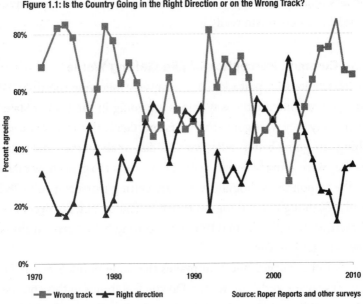

Figure 1.1: Is the Country Going in the Right Direction or on the Wrong Track?

improving in each of fourteen different areas spanning public life,[5] including moral standards, the criminal justice system, public safety, family life, national leaders, Americans' honesty, Americans' work ethic, the health care system, education, our standard of living, the economy, and racial issues. With each one of these issues, about one-quarter to one-half of Americans thought the nation was "holding steady." Among the respondents who perceived any type of change, however, it was overwhelmingly negative. For every respondent who thought that moral and ethical standards were improving, almost twelve thought they were in decline. For every respondent who thought that the criminal justice system was improving, eight thought it was in decline. The ratio was 1:4 for standard of living and 1:3 for racial tensions.[6]

Even when things are objectively getting better, we still think they are getting worse. A 2003 study by the children's advocacy group Child Trends illustrates our propensity for unwarranted pessimism.[7] Child

Trends wanted to gauge the accuracy of Americans' perceptions of children's well-being. They found that Americans think young people are far worse off than they really are. For example, three-quarters of the Americans surveyed thought the number of children on welfare had increased or remained steady in the previous decade, but in reality it had declined. Ninety percent thought that crime rates among teens had gone up or stayed the same, but those too had decreased. In fact, at the time of the survey, they were at a twenty-five-year low! Likewise, Americans are overly pessimistic about young people's poverty, lack of health insurance, and teenage birth rate. The authors concluded, "Most Americans think that things are getting worse for children and youth, even when notable improvements have occurred." Of course the United States has children living in difficult circumstances, but it isn't as prevalent as we seem to think.

While the United States is the best in the world at some things (e.g., basketball, putting people in prison, and In-N-Out hamburgers), pessimism isn't one of them. In 2010, the Pew Global Attitudes Project surveyed respondents in twenty-two different countries, asking them, "Overall, are you satisfied or dissatisfied with the way things are going in our country today?"[8] As plotted in Figure 1.2, the United States is just middle-of-the-pack. In all but one of the nations queried, about half or more of citizens are dissatisfied with the way things are going in their countries, and in most countries two-thirds or more of citizens are dissatisfied. The most dissatisfied country was Lebanon. (National motto: "We don't want to be here either.") The most satisfied, far and away, was China. (National motto: "All 1.3 billion of us are doing quite well. Thank you for asking.") Only 9% of the Chinese were dissatisfied with their country's direction.[9]

The Optimism Gap

At this point, you might be thinking that most humans (except the Chinese) are just pessimistic by nature, but this is not the case.

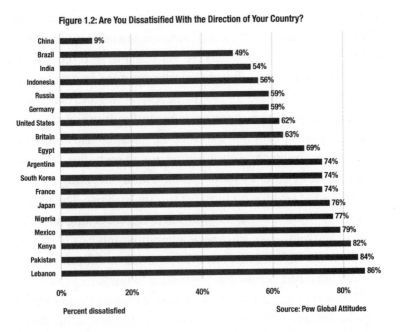

Figure 1.2: Are You Dissatisfied With the Direction of Your Country?

Percent dissatisfied   Source: Pew Global Attitudes

We're actually quite optimistic about our own lives. This personal optimism sets up a paradox in that we think our own lives are going well, but we're convinced that almost everyone else is doing poorly. Basically, we are exceptions to the rule when it comes to life getting worse. Writer David Whitman labels this phenomenon the "optimism gap," and with it we tend to think that the grass is browner, not greener, in other people's yards. Psychologist Fathali Moghaddam characterizes this optimism gap as our thinking that the sky is falling, just not on us.[10]

This optimism gap is demonstrated in a variety of studies. Survey researchers sometimes collect data using what they call the "ladder of life." This type of question asks respondents to rate some aspect of life on a 0-to-10 scale, with 0 representing the worst possible and 10 the best possible. Starting in 1959, the Gallup poll, and later the Pew Foundation, has used this tool to have Americans rate their own life situations as well as the United States as a whole.[11] If the optimism gap did not exist, we would expect these two questions to yield similar results, but that is not the case. As shown in Figure 1.3, in 1959, Americans rated both their personal lives and the nation's condition at the same, relatively high level (6.6 and 6.7 out of 10, respectively). From then on, however, the scores started to diverge, and over the past forty-five years, Americans have consistently rated their own lives better than the nation as a whole. This difference exists both when times are bad, as with the low rating in the early 1970s, and when times are good, as in the mid-1990s. Most recently, in 2008, the average rating for one's own life was 6.8 while for the country it was 5.8. I suppose that I manifest this optimism gap myself. If I had to rate my own life, I would give it an 8, but I'd only give the nation as a whole a 7.

The optimism gap was also found in an intriguing historical study. In the 1980s, journalism professor Nicholas Lemann found

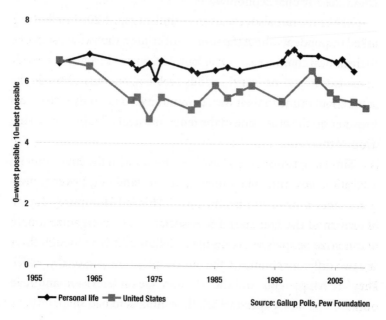

Figure 1.3: How Would You Rate Your Personal Life Situation? The Nation?

Source: Gallup Polls, Pew Foundation

an archive of photographs taken in the 1940s. He tracked down many of the people in those photographs and interviewed them. Almost to a person they reported that their lives had gotten better since the photographs were taken forty years prior, but the great majority of them thought that American life, as a whole, had gone downhill during that same period.[12]

The optimism gap also shows itself with specific issues. Since the early 1970s, the General Social Survey has asked Americans if their financial situation over recent years is getting better, worse, or staying about the same. Similarly, various national surveys have asked the same question about the national economy. Figure 1.4 plots the percentage of Americans who think that their own finances are getting better versus those who think the same about the economy. In every year but one, between 30% and 45% of respondents reported improvement in their own financial situation.[13] In contrast, in most years, only 5% to 25% said the same about the national economy.

The crime rate also reveals an optimism gap. A 2007 Gallup poll asked respondents about the severity of crime nationwide compared to their local community.[14] Over half, 57%, viewed crime nationwide as an "extremely" or "very" serious problem, but only 15% said the same about crime in their own community. So not only is the grass browner on the other side of the fence, but a lot of bullets are flying around there too.

Similar optimism gaps have been found with the environment, education, governmental officials, moral standards, poverty, hunger, homelessness, and health care.[15] This led Humphrey Taylor, chairman of the Lou Harris & Associates survey organization, to summarize people's views on life as follows: "It is as though there are two different countries, the one people know personally, which they are happy with, and the one they see on television and read about in the newspapers, which they think is in bad shape."[16]

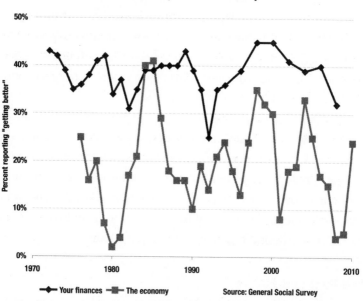

Figure 1.4: Are Your Finances Getting Better? Is the Economy?

Your finances ◆ The economy ■   Source: General Social Survey

Once you start paying attention to it, you'll be surprised at how often you witness this optimism gap in everyday life. For example, earlier this year I was asked to record my first book, *Christians are Hate-Filled Hypocrites... And Other Lies You've Been Told*, as an audio book. I spent several days at a recording studio and got to know the two young guys who owned it. At one point one of them asked me about my next book. When I told him that it examines whether the world is getting better or worse, he laughed and responded, "What could possibly be getting better?" He said this despite the fact that though only in his late twenties, he owns a successful business, drives a Mercedes, is happily married with a child on the way, and seems to be doing pretty well all around. How can he think the world is spiraling downward when his own life is going so well? The optimism gap.

Why does the optimism gap exist?[17] Americans generally have positive views toward their own lives.[18] We value self-esteem, and we display higher levels of it than citizens of other countries, such as China and Japan, who are raised to be more humble and self-effacing. Also, we might give less attention to local problems that affect us personally because they might be too frightening, whereas catching up on bad news someplace else in the world can take on a more recreational form.

This book closes the optimism gap by providing a more accurate—and in many cases more positive—view of what's going on in the world. It occurs to me, however, that another way to close this gap would be to write a book convincing you that your life is worse than you realize. Chapter 1: "Your family: They don't like you either." Chapter 2: "The nice stuff you own: Somebody is going to take it." But I think I'll stick with my original plan.

The Past and Future

Survey questions routinely ask Americans how they perceive the past and the future, and one thing is clear: both are better than the present—at least when we evaluate our nation. A 2009 study asked Americans how things are going in the United States now compared to five years ago, and only 5% of Americans said things now are better. Eighty-three percent said worse, and 10% said about the same.[19] When asked to give their impressions of recent decades, Americans have an unfavorable opinion about their current decade. Fifty-seven percent of respondents in another 2009 study had a favorable opinion of the 1990s, 56% did of the 1980s, 40% the 1970s, and 34% the 1960s. When asked about the year 2000, only 27% had a positive impression of it.[20]

Likewise, Americans tend to be relatively optimistic about the future, though perceptions of the future vary from year to year. In a 2008 poll, 39% of Americans said that the United States would be better off in five years, compared to 34% who said it would be worse. Just one year later, in 2009, 61% said it would be better, versus 19% who said it would be worse.[21] A 2010 Gallup poll asked Americans about different aspects of American life and whether these aspects would be better, worse, or about the same in twenty years. Respondents were most optimistic about the future regarding national security, Americans' hard work, race relations, health, and health care. They had mixed feelings about future standards of living and the functioning of democracy, and they reported pessimism about only one issue: the state of moral values.[22]

Our good feelings about the future come with a hitch: The future never arrives. Surveys have asked questions about the present and the future for several decades now, allowing us to compare Americans' expectations for a specific year in the future versus their feelings about it once it arrives—but the future never seems to live up to its advanced billing. For example, a 1997 survey asked Americans to rate their current quality of life on a ladder scale of 1 to 10, and they averaged a rating of 7. The same survey asked what they expected for five years from then, and they rated their projected quality of life as 8.2. However, when the year 2002 actually rolled around five years later, another survey asked the same questions, and it found that Americans rated the quality of their current lives at just 6.9, but, again, respondents were optimistic about five years into the future, rating it at 8.3.[23] As phrased by a Pew report, the "future ain't what it used to be."[24]

Failed Prophecies of Doom

While rank-and-file Americans are modestly optimistic about the future, journalists, academics, and other experts seem to be more negative overall. In fact, forecasting doom is a viable career strategy, complete with strong book sales, frequent media appearances, and the occasional Nobel Prize. In this section I review a couple of the better-known prophecies of doom. It's kind of fun to see experts be so wrong, an intellectual schadenfreude[25]—rejoicing in others' misfortune. Perhaps more important, realizing the errors of previous, widely accepted prophecies of doom should make us a little more skeptical about current ones, many of which could well turn out to be equally preposterous.

Perhaps the best known historical gloom-and-doomer was Thomas Malthus, an influential British scholar and Anglican clergyman born in 1766. Malthus predicted that the human population would continue to grow until it exceeded the availability of natural resources needed to keep humans alive, thus resulting in a "Malthusian" crisis of famine, poverty, and vice. According to Malthus, humanity could look forward to a continual cycle of population growth followed by social collapse. This prediction did not come about for two reasons: the human population hasn't grown as fast as Malthus expected, and agricultural productivity has increased even faster—making today's world the best fed in human history (as we'll discover in chapter 5).

In recent years, however, the King of Doom has been Paul Ehrlich. Ehrlich is a biologist at Stanford University who originally trained in the study of butterflies, but he transitioned to human ecology. Though most popular in the 1970s and 1980s, his work is still influential. Ehrlich has taken an updated Malthusian approach, linking sustainability to three factors: population size, affluence, and technology. He identifies larger, more affluent, and more technically advanced societies as using more natural resources than other societies, and since societies worldwide are moving toward affluence and growth, he views the world as headed toward scarcity.[26] Based on this perspective, Ehrlich made the following predictions in the 1970s and 1980s, which I'll present along with what really happened.

Hunger:

- *Ehrlich:* "The battle to feed humanity is over. In the 1970s the world will undergo famines. Hundreds of millions of people will starve to death."[27]

- *What happened:* The percentage of people starving world-wide has dropped from 38% in 1970 to 18% in 2001.[28]

India:

- "India couldn't possibly feed two hundred million more people by 1980," or "be self-sufficient in food by 1971."[29]
- India has grown to over one billion people, and their average caloric intake is 50% higher than in the 1950s.[30]

Commodities:

- "Before 1985, mankind will enter a genuine age of scarcity in which many things besides energy will be in short supply. . . . Such diverse commodities as food, fresh water, copper, and paper will become increasingly difficult to obtain and thus much more expensive."[31]
- Most commodities are cheaper and more widely available now than ever.[32]

Life expectancy:

- "The U.S. life expectancy will drop to forty-two years by 1980, due to cancer epidemics."[33]
- American life expectancy has steadily risen in past decades, and now it's at about seventy-eight years.[34]

Air pollution:

- "Smog disasters in 1973 might kill 200,000 people in New York and Los Angeles."[35]
- The air in Los Angeles, New York, and most American cities is substantially cleaner now than in the 1970s.[36]

And my personal favorite:

- "I would take even money that England will not exist in the year 2000."[37]
- I have it on good authority that England is still there.

How wrong was Ehrlich with these predictions? As my seventeen-year-old son, Gus,[38] would say, Ehrlich was "epic-ally" wrong. Yet many people believed Ehrlich back then and many still do. Over the summer, I was asked by a publisher to review a forthcoming textbook for introductory sociology. It had a chapter on the environment, and its primary source was Paul Ehrlich and his Malthusian vision, written as if it were still the early 1970s.

As an aside, one can only hope that Ehrlich himself experienced an optimism gap, feeling better about his own life than the world as a whole. Can you imagine otherwise? "Hey, Paul, want to eat out tonight?" "No, thanks, the restaurants are probably out of food and there might be food riots." "Okay. How about a drive?" "No, we'll probably choke to death on smog while caught in traffic jams." "Hmm, how about a trip to England?"

Paul Ehrlich wasn't the first, nor will he be the last, expert to get these things terribly wrong. In 1980, a lengthy governmental report entitled "The Global 2000 Report to the President" presented the predictions of leading experts of the day about what will happen in the future, and things weren't looking so good. They summarized their predictions as follows:

> If present trends continue, the world in 2000 will be more crowded, more polluted, less stable ecologically, and more vulnerable to disruption than the world we live in now. Serious stresses involving population, resources, and environment are clearly visible ahead. Despite greater material output, the world's people will be poorer in many ways than they are today. . . . Barring revolutionary advances in technology, life

for most people on earth will be more precarious in 2000 than it is now.[39]

As we will see throughout this book, few of these expectations have come to pass.

Malthus, Ehrlich, and Global 2000 are far from the only doom-sayers. A 1994 *Atlantic Monthly* article predicted "scarcity, crime, overpopulation, tribalism, and disease that would destroy the fabric of our planet."[40] A bestselling book of that time warned that "perhaps hundreds of millions of people would soon die in unstoppable pandemics of mutant diseases, such as Ebola."[41] A well-known futurist has predicted that the United States is headed for food riots and Central Park will be engulfed by shantytowns.[42]

The High Cost of Unwarranted Pessimism

If this were just an academic exercise, then our perceptions of the world might not really matter, but it's more than that. In various ways, our negatively skewed understanding of the world causes real problems.

The prevailing view that most everything is getting worse makes it difficult to prioritize, since we don't know what is *actually* getting worse. If everything is a problem, then, in a sense, nothing is. David Whitman put it: "False alarms drive out true ones."[43] Our fear of plane accidents might blind us to the reality that driving to the airport is actually more dangerous than flying.[44] Similarly, the steady stream of fear messages about the environment can lead us to incorrectly prioritizing environmental problems.[45] This incorrect prioritization literally can be a life-and-death matter. For example, in the 1990s, AIDS activists sought to raise concern about the disease, so they emphasized heterosexuals' potential risk of contracting it, even though it struck mostly gay men. As a result of this distortion of risk, government agencies shifted their focus to AIDS prevention among straight people—at the cost of giving it to the more needy gays. In California, from 1989 to 1992, only 9% of AIDS prevention funds targeted gay men despite the fact that they constituted 85% of all AIDS cases.[46] This incorrect prioritization probably cost lives.

Viewing the world as getting worse also casts doubt on the efficacy of proposed programs and policies to make things better. If everything is getting worse, then the solutions imposed in the past didn't work, so why should we have faith in today's solutions? In general, fear messages are a good short-term strategy for getting people to act, but they are less effective over the long term because they disillusion and discourage.[47] In fact, consistently pessimistic messages about the world can become self-fulfilling prophecies. Hearing that a problem has steadily gotten worse, despite our past efforts to alleviate it, might be enough to make us want to stop trying. Many advocacy groups use pessimistic, fearful messages to raise awareness for their cause, which ironically can actually reduce their effectiveness, as people stop believing they can change the situation. A spokesperson for Greenpeace acknowledged this when he lamented that the constant pessimism put out by environmental groups actually weakens their credibility as the public hears it year after year.[48]

Viewing the world as getting worse also bears personal costs. A Mayo Clinic report found that a pessimistic view of life can harm many areas of health and well-being.[49] In particular, constant negative thinking can result in a shorter life-span, increased depression and distress, less resistance to the common cold, worse psychological and physical well-being, increased risk of cardiovascular disease, and diminished coping skills during times of stress. Other studies have linked a negative outlook on life to mild cognitive impairment as well as Alzheimer's disease.[50] This doesn't mean that we're all one Greenpeace report away from falling over dead, but rather that the barrage of negative news about the world cannot be good for us.

To be clear, my concerns are with unwarranted pessimism, not all pessimism. Pessimism, if accurate, can serve us well, and ignoring real problems has its own costs. Accurate perceptions of the world, both in the ways that it's getting better and worse, is the ideal.

The Plan of This Book

The goal of this book is not to comprehensively review every single issue facing Americans (that might take two books), but rather to focus on a limited set of issues that I believe are important to most people. Obviously, I judge what is important from my own particular social location. Hopefully most of the topics I cover will strike readers as significant, but some may not. Not only do I examine health, income, wars, and the environment—widely agreed-upon "big" issues—I also explore various less-agreed-upon issues. For example, some people define premarital sex as a social problem, while others think it's not a big deal. My own take on this issue, as well as others', is informed by my Christian faith, so if you do not share my values, as—gasp—some people don't, you might find some issues less compelling than I do.[51]

There are, of course, many, many issues from which to choose, each with copious amounts of available data. Writing this book was like trying to fill a coffee mug from a fire hydrant—there is almost too much information. In fact, my biggest frustration in writing was figuring out how to prune major topics down to several pages of information. I had to drop a lot of elaboration and nuance about each topic in order to highlight its core findings and still leave room to explore other topics. Consider, for example, the annual Health Report from the U.S. Centers for Disease Control and Prevention. It contains over five hundred pages of detailed information about health trends in the United States. The index alone is eleven pages! In it you can learn about rates of triplets, dental visits, lower back pain, whooping cough, organ transplants, and hundreds of other health-related issues. Every one of these health issues is of importance, but

I couldn't possibly cover all of them. When it comes to health, I examine only several of what I deem to be the most important issues, including longevity, major diseases, hunger, and substance abuse.

Evaluating the problems facing society at any given time is inherently subjective. It's natural for people to arbitrarily judge the current situation of an issue as either good or bad. For example, as of 2007, 24% of Americans smoke cigarettes.[52] Is this number acceptable, too high, or too low? There is often no objective definition of problems; rather, they are open to subjective judgment, and two people can look at the same data and come to very different conclusions. One could say the cup is half full, and the other might say, "Hey, that's not my drink."

This book shies away from evaluating current levels of any given issue, and instead focuses on change over time. Is a particular issue getting worse, better, or staying about the same? Advantageously, this approach is reasonably objective, and all parties on a given issue should be able to agree on how it is changing (assuming suitable data).[53] For example, fewer Americans smoke today than in 1965, when 42% smoked; this is true whether you're a tobacco company executive or an anti-smoking activist.

Nonetheless, even trends over time are also subject to subjective evaluation. Just because something is getting better doesn't necessarily mean that it's getting better fast enough to suit people. We can see substantial progress and still want much more. As former president Bill Clinton once said, "The crime rate is down, the welfare rolls are down, the food stamp rolls are down, the teen pregnancy rate is down . . . And yet, we all know that all those things that are going down are still too high."[54] Such ethical judgments are part of living in society, but I don't emphasize them. Instead, I focus on describing how things are changing, and others can debate whether these changes are enough.

The main focus of this book is tracking changes over time, but with some issues I also describe differences between groups—especially when people's experiences with an issue vary widely. With the United States, I highlight differences based on gender, race and ethnicity, class, age, and other social fault lines. With the world, I compare countries or regions to underscore international differences.

Going into this book I didn't have strong preconceptions about whether the world is getting better or worse; I treated this book as a chance to learn about it myself. My goal here is accuracy, and I tried to go wherever the data took me. Ultimately, I conclude that many things in the world are indeed getting better, but I did not set out to write a "positive" book. Indeed, this book catalogues issues that are getting better as well as some that are getting worse. Writer Robert Samuelson underscores the importance of this approach when he writes:

> We'd be better off with a more balanced view of our present
> condition. We need a clearer understanding of our strengths
> and shortcomings, because we are ill served by either excessive
> optimism or excessive pessimism. The first regularly leads us
> into romantic schemes that are doomed to fail, while the second
> may condemn us to hopelessness and continued paralysis.[55]

The meat of this book is statistical description. Surveys, census data, and other sources provide rich and accurate descriptions of the population as a whole. However, sometimes we lose the power of individual actions and local situations when we rely solely on statistical data. To counter this, and to provide a richer understanding of changes in the world, I also include stories that highlight unique, altruistic contributions made by people trying to improve the world. One of the conclusions of this book is that the world is improving so much because so many people are working to make it a better place. To help us appreciate the impact of this altruism, I tell some of their stories.

CHAPTER 2

WHY ARE WE SO SURE THINGS ARE GOING DOWNHILL?

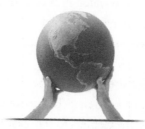

How do we explain that people are "doing better but feeling worse about society"?

—*Aaron Wildavsky, political scientist*[1]

While the quality of life is improving, the main message of the media is that it's getting worse, told over and over again, in a thousand separate stories.

—*Ben Wattenberg, television commentator*[2]

The humour of blaming the present, and admiring the past, is strongly rooted in human nature, and has an influence even on persons endued with the profoundest judgment and most extensive learning.

—*David Hume, philosopher*[3]

Why are we so pessimistic about the current state of our nation and our world? Scholars have offered various explanations to help us understand why we fear what we fear today and what we might fear tomorrow.

Media

The media sells negative worldviews. It's not that reporters, writers, and editors are pessimistic people; rather, they have a strong incentive to tell us about the fearful, scary, and dangerous happenings in our world. The media is a business, and it succeeds by attracting viewers and readers. With hundreds of television channels and even more online news sources, how can they do this? One way is to offer something that is truly frightening. If watching a story can save us from some imminent danger, then maybe we'll stop channel surfing long enough to watch it. If reading a report can protect us from a health scare, maybe we'll pick the magazine off the rack. Sensationalism and fear sells—this is a fact of life that won't change anytime soon.[4]

This "incentive for the negative" means that bad news will be emphasized more than good news.[5] To illustrate, in 1994, at the peak of the AIDS epidemic, the Centers for Disease Control and Prevention (CDC) published a report that AIDS deaths had increased that year, and the *New York Times* gave this report extensive coverage. The next year, however, the CDC announced that the number of AIDS diagnoses had fallen, and the *Times* effectively ignored this information.[6]

In a similar vein, in 2008, public health professor Seymour Garte attended a conference about the environment, and he heard a conference speaker state that air pollution has steadily dropped in the United States and Europe. (We'll learn more about this in chapter 10.) Garte looked around the room to see how other people reacted to this statement—and the experts in the field readily accepted it. It surprised Garte, however, because he had "never seen it published in the media."[7]

Even when things are going well, we still hear predominately bad news. A study in the 1980s compared economic measures with how they were reported. At the time, the economy was doing well, and about 95% of the economic measures were positive (e.g., economic growth, declining unemployment). You might assume that since the economy was doing so well, most of the news stories about it would be positive. Um, were you born yesterday? In this time of economic prosperity, 85% of the economic stories on network television were negative.[8]

Here's another way to appreciate the negative slant of most media—compare it to news sources that explicitly emphasize good news. There aren't many of them, but they do exist. One of them is the Good News Network Web site, and here are some of its recent headlines:

- "Good News About the Aging Brain: The middle-age brain outperforms its younger self in many ways."
- "Australian Angel Preventing Jumps at Suicide Spot"
- "Woman's Wallet Returned With More Money Inside"
- "Green Tea Extract Appears to Keep Cancer in Check"
- "Jennifer Aniston Among Celebs Donating Shoes to Hero in Heels Auction"

Just for comparisons' sake, I went to my local newspaper the same day, and its lead stories included an attempted rape, a teacher arrested for child pornography, traffic accidents, and many other bad things. In fact, I'm so used to a certain style of "bad news" that the "good news" outlets don't feel like "real" news. Jennifer Aniston donating shoes to charity? So what? Jennifer Aniston hitting Angelina Jolie with a shoe? Now that's news!

The media's presentation of the world might actually be getting more negative over time. With countless channels on TV and virtually every newspaper and magazine available online, media is now a hyper-competitive industry. This gives any particular media provider greater incentive to feature more sex, violence, and any other sensationalism that might sell. In contrast, not very long ago, the major media providers had a near monopoly on the market, which enabled them to feature less exciting news than they felt was important for readers and viewers to know.[9]

Commentator Ben Wattenberg has pointed out that the media can find bad news even in good news—that any story can be spun negatively.[10] In short, even silver clouds have dark linings when the media deals with them. Here are some examples of how any issue can be described negatively:

- Life expectancy. If life expectancy decreases, people are dying younger. If it increases, it strains the social security system.
- Disease. An unpreventable disease harms people; a preventable disease means disparities in access to medical treatment.
- Fertility. High birthrates cause overcrowding; low birthrates cause school closings and lowered future tax revenues.
- Oil prices. High prices increase the cost of living; low prices result in bankruptcies and unemployment among oil companies.

I'm not advocating that the media spurn all negative reporting in favor of good news, for our society does have its problems. As former Senator Daniel Moynihan pointed out, "If you come into a country and all you see in the paper is good news—then all the good people are in jail."[11] I have no worry, however, that the media will overemphasize the positive anytime soon, and we can expect a continued diet of the sinister and despairing.

Advocates

Advocates are another source of bad news. Advocates support a particular cause, and they use facts and arguments to illustrate and support their position (rather than to test if it's true). This selective presentation of information usually means emphasizing what's going wrong or getting worse in order to raise awareness, solicit money, or change public policy. If the media gives us bad news for ratings, then advocates give us bad news for a good cause. More cynically, it has been termed "lying for justice." There is nothing inherently immoral or unethical about advocacy groups' very selective use of facts; instead, we just need to be aware of it.[12] Advancing a cause, and not accuracy per se, is their goal.

Advocates' fixation on the negative is usually clear in how they present information. To illustrate, this morning I took a look at Greenpeace's Web site, and their recent press releases regarded rain forest destruction, chemical disasters, toxic computers, and oil spills. The sidebar contained links for donating money and volunteering with Greenpeace to deal with these problems.

From an advocate's perspective, good news—even if factually correct—can be harmful. In the 1980s, homeless advocates claimed that a half million to 2 million Americans were homeless. Peter Rossi, a distinguished survey researcher, conducted a rigorous count of the number of homeless people in Chicago and used this number to estimate the homeless population nationwide. This more systematic approach produced an estimate of about 150,000 to 200,000 homeless people—about one-third that of the lowest estimate previously used by advocates. Homeless advocates were greatly upset with Rossi's study, even though it was ostensibly good news, because they feared that it would undercut their ability to get funding for homeless people. They accused Rossi of everything from incompetence to mean-spiritedness. Rossi, who himself had been very active in helping homeless people, concluded from the situation that "no good applied social research goes unpunished."[13]

More recently, Alan Lopez of Queensland University in Australia published a paper revising how to calculate the number of infant deaths worldwide. Using a probably-more-accurate method, he estimates 8 million infant deaths, lower than the previous estimate of 8.8 million. A decrease of 800,000 children dying is wonderful news, but when he presented his work to a conference of health officials, they did not cheer him on, carrying him around the room on their shoulders while chanting his name. No, instead they fretted that this reappraisal would diminish the perceived importance of the problem and make it harder for them to raise money and public support for their cause.[14]

In short, advocates deemphasize social progress because it might stand in the way of their work for . . . social progress.[15] Bjorn Lomborg, whom we will learn more about in chapter 10, is a political scientist-turned-environmentalist. He has written that environmentally, a lot of things are getting better. When he lectures, however, he frequently encounters people who acknowledge that his facts may be correct, but that "such arguments should not be voiced in public as they might cause us to take things a bit too easy."[16] The working assumption of many advocates seems to be that people cannot handle the truth; they need to be duped for their and the world's own good.

It's in predicting the future, more so than describing the present, that we see advocates in their full glory. Since the future has not yet arrived, predictions are essentially educated (or otherwise) guesses. This means that no data exists today to test our predictions about what will happen tomorrow, thus freeing advocates to tell some real whoppers. For example, world leaders got together in 1992 to discuss and sign a document setting the agenda for the future. In it, they wrote that "Humanity stands at a defining moment in history. We are confronted with a perpetuation of disparities within and between nations, a worsening of poverty, hunger, ill health, and illiteracy." In actuality, the following decade saw almost record decreases in poverty, hunger, poor health, and illiteracy.[17] Seymour

Garte summarizes that "according to many environmentalists of the 1960s and 1970s, by now we should all be either dead or living in a horrible world without light, air, or natural resources."[18]

Anecdotes and Bad Statistics

If bad news accompanies even accurate data, how much more will it with inaccurate, substandard, or otherwise misleading data? Take anecdotes and examples (for example). When a news story covers a particular issue, reporters will often highlight the most extreme— and negative—example of it. The resulting story is then used to define the larger pattern.[19] Powerful examples easily overwhelm the actual facts, so we understand the world based on worst-case scenarios rather than a systematic study of actual trends and patterns.[20] As psychologist David Myers puts it, "With apologies to Mark Twain, there are three kinds of lies—lies, damn lies, and vivid but misleading anecdotes. One can marshal dramatic stories to support any contention, or its opposite."[21]

To illustrate, in 1999, two high school seniors murdered twelve classmates and a teacher at Columbine High School. This made for an extraordinarily powerful example of school violence because it happened in a "normal" middle-class, suburban high school, and there's a media record of it—surveillance footage of the assailants shooting people, recordings of frantic 9-1-1 calls, and interviews with crying survivors. This instance redefined our understanding of school safety; in fact, I even knew families who considered pulling their children from public schools as a result of Columbine. What's the reality? Schools are extraordinarily safe places. There are over 49 million public school students in the U.S., but each year there are fewer than one hundred school-related murders, and there is no evidence that schools are getting more dangerous.[22] In actuality, children are at much greater risk of harm outside of school—at home or on the streets.

Another type of misleading evidence has to do with the statistics themselves. Everything varies in quality. There are good restaurants and bad restaurants, good used cars and bad used cars, good U.S. presidents and bad presidents. Why shouldn't we expect the same with statistics? Sociologist Joel Best classifies the different types of bad statistics as follows: some numbers are bad to begin with; some numbers get bad as they are passed along; and some numbers are chosen because they are bad.

Some of the worst statistics are flat-out made up—as factual as fairy tales. For example, in the 1980s and 1990s, a widely publicized statistic about young people made the rounds. According to this statistic, in a 1940s survey, schoolteachers identified their top problems as children talking and chewing gum in class and running in the hallways. Forty years later, however, their top problems were drug abuse, pregnancy, suicide, and assault. This made a compelling case for the condition of society, but there was just one problem: it was entirely made up. A businessman in Texas, T. Cullen Davis, constructed the list to highlight his perceptions of problems in today's schools. He identified the 1940s problems from his own experiences as a school kid and modern problems from reading the newspaper. Even after this list was exposed as a hoax, it was still cited as factual by government officials.[23]

Would you like another made-up statistic? They are kind of fun, aren't they? Joel Best nominates this one as the worst social statistic ever.[24] Professor Best was reading a student's dissertation prospectus that started with this attention-grabbing line: "Every year since 1950, the number of American children gunned down has doubled." The student drew this statistic from a 1995 article published in an academic journal. What's the problem with this number? Doubling numbers adds up really fast. As Best calculated, if only one American child was murdered in 1950, then it would be two in 1951, four in 1952, eight in 1953, and so on. By 1960, it would be 1,024 murders, and by 1970 it would be one million kids murdered. In 1980 there would be 1 billion children murdered in the United States, and in 1995, the time of the article, the estimate would be 35 trillion children murdered. Wow! Now that would be a problem.

Even when statistics begin their lives as "good" numbers, they can mutate as they are passed along, becoming twisted and distorted with each retelling. A classic statistical mutation regards anorexia nervosa.[25] In the 1980s and 1990s, studies found that up to 150,000 women suffered from anorexia, and it *could* lead to death (though it rarely did). Advocates, wanting to bring attention to this disease, latched on to this statistic. At some point, however, the statistic mutated to 150,000 women *dying* each year from anorexia. In reality, only about one hundred or so women died each year from anorexia, but this wildly inflated statistic made it into influential books and newspaper stories, being cited as truth by well-known figures such as feminists Gloria Steinem and Naomi Wolf, and advice columnist Ann Landers.[26]

Short-Term Fluctuations

Even if by some miracle all the statistics created and disseminated were accurate, we might still hear disproportionately bad news because of the nature of short-term fluctuations. Social change is rarely linear, and even if a long-term trend is positive, it will usually have occasional short-term setbacks. Progress is several steps forward and one step back. These short-term fluctuations, when negative, are often viewed as more interesting and newsworthy, so we hear about them. Because short-term fluctuations receive so much attention, even if we had perfect data about the world, which we don't, and everything were getting better over time, which it isn't, we would still probably think that much of the world is getting worse.

For example, tuberculosis in the United States has declined

substantially over the last century, going from 80 to 90 cases per 100,000 in the 1940s to less than 10 per 100,000 now. However, in the late 1980s, there was a brief, slight rise in tuberculosis cases. This blip, which only lasted a year or two, received lots of attention, and it was interpreted as a reversal in long-term tuberculosis trends. One well-known environmentalist even cited it as evidence of an "ecology of increasing disease."[27]

Nostalgia

Another problem in comparing the past and the present involves nostalgia. We romanticize and long for the past for various reasons. When we were children, our parents protected us from uncomfortable aspects of life, and moral choices seemed more straightforward. Our lives felt simpler, more appealing.[28] This idealization of youth comes through in survey data as well. Surveys have asked people to identify the best decade in recent history, and people usually choose the decade of their teens and twenties. So a forty-year-old today would think fondly of the 1980s, and a sixty-year-old the 1960s. Youth is a relatively carefree time of growth, exploration, and discovery, but by middle-age we are burdened with providing for children, making ends meet, advancing our careers, and planning for retirement.[29] This has certainly been true in my own life. After high school I hitchhiked around Europe for five months. Now, at age forty-seven, I'm lucky to make it as far as the mall by myself. While I make more money now, I somehow had more discretionary income then. Why, if I could still fit into my old disco pants, I might want to go back to the 1970s.

The problem is that nostalgia glosses over the past's problems, and we end up comparing what was good in the past with what is bad today. No wonder we always think life is getting worse. As good as things get now, the past gets better even faster.[30] For example, some Americans view the 1950s as a great time for America—the greatest generation and all that. This nostalgia ignores, however, the harsher realities of that time, including a racially segregated South, the Korean War, an arms race with the Soviet Union, bomb shelter drills, and the polio epidemic.[31] Comedian Jackie Gleason put it this way: "The past remembers better than it lived."[32]

Unrealistic Expectations

If nostalgia inflates the past, unrealistic expectations deflate the present. We as Americans have high—perhaps impossibly high— standards for our society. As Tocqueville observed long ago, Americans believe in "the indefinite perfectibility of man."[33] We idealize what society should be: well-paying secure jobs, racial harmony, high-quality inexpensive health care, enlightened corporations, a generous and effective government, a clean environment, and almost limitless personal freedom and self-fulfillment.[34]

Writer Robert Samuelson makes a strong case that this idealization of society increased substantially after World War II.[35] In the 1950s and 1960s, America experienced a substantial economic boom, transforming society in countless ways and giving us confidence that we could solve any social problem. We declared war on poverty, marched for civil rights, and protested for the environment. Politicians fed our expectations with sky-high promises.[36] We blurred the line between the American Dream and an American fantasy.

The problem arises when our own experiences don't match this idealized society. Any one of us will probably experience hardship, disability, discrimination, or just plain bad luck, and even if things are going well for us, we all know someone who is having a tough time. We hear of crime, poverty, unemployment, homelessness, the uninsured, and corporate failures. These problems unnerve us because we imagine, and even expect, a country without them, and this can lead us to evaluate society negatively.[37] By not distinguishing between progress and perfection, we can become skeptical and disillusioned about the world. Writer Greg Easterbrook comments that should the paradise of Eden ever be restored here on earth, we would probably complain about the menu of milk and honey being too predictable and the friendly lions roaring too loudly.[38]

Christians: The Bad News and Hastening Jesus' Return

We Christians have additional reasons for hearing and embracing bad news. Christian pastors, writers, speakers, and others who communicate the gospel often portray it as a solution to a problem, both for individual people and society as a whole. As part of the presentation, they often motivate the need for this solution by describing how bad things have become. Negative, fearful, and sensationalistic stories of the world can be used to underscore the need for the gospel.[39] As a result, active Christians are exposed to an extra dose of pessimism.

Theologically, Christian belief entails the world coming to an end with the second coming of Christ. The end times have been given various descriptions, but they usually involve severe worldwide problems. These problems include social chaos, the demise of the family, the overturning of traditional economic and social structures, environmental degradation, and the collapse of society itself. Christians might be especially likely to accept a pessimistic view of the world's condition, for it fits with our theology.

Historian Paul Boyer offers various examples of Christians linking the world's problems to the Second Coming. Billy Graham cited environmental problems such as famine, ecological degradation, pollution, and the nuclear threat as indicative of the end times. The pestilences prophesied by Jesus, he wrote, may be a sign of the end of time and "may . . . have to do with man's poisoning of his environment through massive industrialization."[40] In a similar vein, popular Christian author David Wilkerson interpreted the horrible sores mentioned in the book of Revelation to increased solar radiation. He wrote: "Revelation 16 actually describes effects now being attributed to the hole in the Ozone Layer."[41]

Regardless of how or why the bad news comes to us, the real issue is separating fact from fiction. The rest of the book is my attempt to do just that. Be warned: surprises lie ahead.

ARE WE WORSE OFF FINANCIALLY THAN WE USED TO BE?

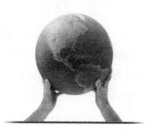

The twentieth century was, with the notable exception of the 1930s, one of prodigious economic advancement in America. While working fewer hours, Americans easily quadrupled their real earnings.

—*Claude Fischer and Michael Hout, sociologists*[1]

If we revisit America before the Second World War, even briefly, we find a country that seems almost primitive by present standards.
—*Robert Samuelson, writer*[2]

We need to save more money and take on less debt.
—*Economic Report to the President, 2010*[3]

I begin this chapter with a test. (I am a professor, so I do this to people.) Here are twelve generalizations about the economic situation in the United States. Which are true and which are false?

- Americans' living standards have been falling since the early 1970s.
- The rich get richer, the poor get poorer, and most of us are getting nowhere.
- Life is getting harder; we're working more, and there's never enough time to enjoy life.
- Both adults have to work these days to maintain a family's standard of living.
- Because Americans' incomes are falling, the United States is no longer the Land of Opportunity, particularly for the less educated.
- Despite decades of affirmative action and moral persuasion, women and minorities are falling further behind.
- Employment prospects are bleak because good jobs are being destroyed as companies lay off workers to boost profits and splurge on executive pay.
- American workers are no longer as productive as they once were.
- As companies ship our high-paying manufacturing jobs overseas, the U.S. is left with inferior service jobs, condemning the country to become a nation of hamburger flippers.
- The current generation of children may be the first in history not to live as well as their parents.
- America's economic fortunes will erode further because the country isn't fit to compete in the high-technology world of the future.

The answer? According to Federal Reserve Bank economists W. Michael Cox and David Alm, all twelve of these commonly accepted economic beliefs are false.[4]

Income in the U.S.

Let's start with income—the way most of us get money. How are Americans doing with income? The answer: amazing over the past century, but just okay over the past decade. Figure 3.1 plots Americans' median yearly income since 1947 (adjusted for inflation).[5] There are three lines on the figure: one representing changes in family income and the other two the incomes of men and women who work full time year-round. As you can see, today's families earn more money than did families in the 1940s. How much more? A lot more. In the late 1940s, the median family income was about $25,000 a year. Now it's over $60,000 a year—a full 240% increase! (Again, these numbers are adjusted for inflation). Now, I'm not sure, but I guess that if your boss offered to double your salary and then increase it by another 40%, you would say yes, perhaps without even giving it much thought. Well, that's basically what's happened to American family income over the past sixty years.

From the 1940s through the early 1970s, Americans' incomes grew at a dizzying rate. American family income doubled from the quarter century between 1947 and 1973, but it increased only 20% in the next twenty-five years, through 1999. The growth in family income slowed down in the 1970s mainly because men's incomes flattened out. As shown in Figure 3.1, male workers have earned about the same amount of money over the last thirty-five years.[6] Why, then, did family incomes continue to increase? More women worked outside the house, and they worked longer hours. In 1960, just over 40% of adult women worked in the labor force, but by 2000 it was about 75%.[7] Women's income has steadily increased over the past fifty years, thus boosting total family income.[8]

Starting in 1999, however, Americans' family income stopped growing, staying at about $62,000. Since three-quarters of adult women already work, economists don't expect many more women to go off to work, so future increases in family income will have to

Figure 3.1: Americans' Family and Individual Income Levels

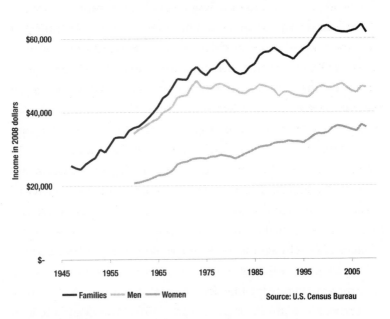

Families — Men — Women   Source: U.S. Census Bureau

come from overall increases in individual earnings. In short, we're running out of family members to send to work.[9] (Maybe kids are next?) While the average income across all families has remained about the same, the incomes of any particular family has probably increased over time as family members earn more money with age due to raises, promotions, and getting better jobs. In other words, even if all American families earn about the same now as a decade ago, your family probably makes more now than it did then.

Income isn't the only benefit provided by employment. Employment can also provide health care, retirement, maternity leave, and stock options, and these benefits can be of great value. Fringe benefits save us money because we spend less of our own money on things like medical expenses and retirement. For example, my own health insurance requires only a small co-pay for doctor's visits, hospital stays, and prescriptions. This gives us peace of mind, knowing that we can get medical care when we need it—without regard to its financial costs. Fortunately, employers have provided more and more fringe benefits over time. Economists Cox and Alm estimate that the value of fringe benefits increased by one-third from 1970 to the 1990s alone.[10] As such, total compensation, i.e., income plus fringe benefits, has risen more than income by itself. When fringe benefits are added to the equation, total compensation rose by nearly one-third from 1980 to 2004.[11]

Another change relevant to understanding income involves family sizes. Over the past several decades, families have gotten smaller. In 1970, the average household had four people; now it's down to 2.5.[12] This means that even if family income levels have hit a plateau, income per person has continued to increase. From 1970 to 2006, family income—regardless of family size—increased 23%. However, this number is bigger when we adjust for family size. For example, a family of four today actually earns 41% more than a family of four in 1970.[13]

While formal work is the main source of money for most people, it's not the only source. We can also get money from gifts, earn it in the informal economy (and usually not report it to the government), earn interest on our investments, receive government benefits, and borrow against the value of our home. It's difficult to measure each of these other sources of money directly, so economists use an indirect measure to capture all the money taken in by Americans—personal consumption; i.e., how much money people spend on goods and services. Over the long term, Americans' personal consumption has risen dramatically. From 1929 to 2004, it went from about $5,000 to $25,000 per person (measured in year-2000 dollars, thus controlling for inflation).[14] Even in recent decades it has gone up 74% (again, adjusted for inflation).[15] This suggests that even as income from formal work has leveled out, we still have more and more money to spend.

In any discussion of income, it's important to recognize gender differences. The most commonly cited statistic about this usually takes the following form: Women earn x% as much as men for the same work, with the x being usually between 60% and 80%. As shown in Figure 3.1, the income levels of men and women who work full time are coming together over time, meaning that the gender difference in income is lessening. In the 1960s, full-time women workers made about 60% of what men earned, but now it's 77%. Furthermore, as discussed earlier, women's average earnings have increased in recent decades whereas men's have not.

How do we interpret this gender difference? Some view it as entirely due to discrimination—almost as if a company's payroll person notices that a worker wears a skirt and then deducts 23% from her pay. In reality, the gender difference is more difficult to interpret. There is actually little income difference by gender when two conditions are met: men and women work the same job, and they have similar qualifications. For example, economists Marianne Bertrand and Kevin Hallock examined the pay of high-level business executives, and they found that women executives earned only 65% that of male executives.[16] However, about three-fourths of this difference resulted from the women working at smaller companies, which pay less. The rest of the difference was mostly due to the women being younger and having less seniority. Similarly, young male physicians earn 41% more than do female physicians, but this is almost entirely due to their working in higher-paying medical specialties.[17]

But this still leaves room for discrimination, for perhaps women are guided to lower-paying jobs. Here is an example from my family history. My mother and her brother (my uncle) both wanted to become physicians when they graduated from college in the 1950s. My mother, however, was told that it wasn't a suitable career for a woman, so she worked as a chemist. My uncle, however, ended up becoming the president of the American College of Surgeons. In the same vein, it could be that women are promoted less often than men. The Bertrand and Hallock study found that only 2.5% of top executives were women. It's hard for me to imagine that for every forty men promoted to executive, there is only one qualified woman.

Another possible source of discrimination regards how much is paid for different types of jobs. Perhaps society devalues predominately female jobs, so these jobs pay less. Typically "women's" jobs pay less than "men's" jobs. Jobs like bank teller, nurse, secretary, housecleaner, and elementary school teacher are important, but they don't pay as well as "men's" jobs, such as bank manager, construction worker, doctor, and mechanic.

So is there gender discrimination in earnings? It's hard to know with certainty, given the multiple reasons why men earn more money than women. I suspect that not all gender difference in earnings results from discrimination, but by the same token there is enough smoke that makes it hard to believe there's not also some fire. What we know with certainty is that gender inequality has steadily decreased, suggesting the same for the discrimination that it implies.[18]

Income Around the Globe

When we examine income levels around the world, it is remarkable how much variation exists between countries. In some countries people have a lot of money, and in other countries they have next to nothing. Data from the World Bank indicates about a dozen countries in which residents have average annual incomes of $40,000 or more. These include Kuwait, Norway, Singapore, the United States, Hong Kong, Switzerland, the Netherlands, and, at the top, Luxemburg, with over $57,000.[19] (Country motto: "Yeah, we're small, but check out the size of our paychecks.") At the poor end of the scale are the many countries that average less than $1,000 a year. These include Guinea, Ethiopia, Mozambique, Sierra Leone, Central African Republic, Congo, and, coming in last, Liberia at $290 a year.

Whole regions of the world vary widely in income. As a reference point, here in the United States we average about $47,000 a year per person. Europe, as a whole, averages about $36,000. Central Asia averages about $13,000; Latin America and the Caribbean $10,000; North Africa and the Middle East $8,000; East Asia and the Pacific $6,000; and at the bottom, Sub-Saharan Africa at $2,000. When you go to the bookstore or listen to the radio or watch television, there are a lot of people giving advice on how to make money, but they usually overlook the single most important factor: be born in the right place.

Across almost all countries, income has risen substantially over the last two centuries. Figure 3.2 plots per-person income levels since the year 1800, and one of the big winners is the United States.[20] In the year 1820, Americans earned an average of $2,000 a year per person (in inflation-adjusted, 2008 dollars). By 1950 it was over $15,000, and by 2001 it was $45,000. Other regions have witnessed substantial raises. Latin America, for example, averaged $1,000 per person in 1820, $4,000 in 1950, and $9,000 in 2001. Russia had a similar trend, going from $1,000 to $4,500 to $7,000 (although it dropped somewhat after the collapse of the USSR). China's per-capita income in 1800 was $950 and only $700 in 1950, but it has since exploded, increasing eightfold to almost $6,000. India has tripled its average income over the past fifty years. Even Africa increased its per-capita income 350% since 1820.

Angus Maddison, a British economist, has put together a fascinating data set that tracks income trends over the past two thousand years. He gathered his data from official documents, personal letters, trade records, and whatever other source he could find.[21] According to Maddison, in the first millennium after Christ—through the year 1000—most of the world was poor by today's standards—living on little more than a dollar a day ($400 to $600 a year). Things picked up

Figure 3.2: World Income

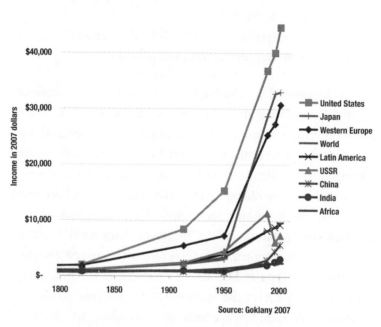

Source: Goklany 2007

in the next millennium. From the year 1000 to 1820, world income levels slowly crawled upward, increasing about 50% over this eight-hundred-year span. Starting in about 1820, world per-capita income shot up dramatically, such that over the past millennium, world income rates increased by thirteen-fold (i.e., 1,300%).[22] Read that sentence again—it's remarkable. Even since 1955, just fifty years ago, the world income has increased three-fold (i.e., 300%).[23] This means that worldwide, our grandparents' generation lived on about one-third of what we do.

This raises an obvious question: What happened in 1820 to bring such a dramatic change in income? Being curious in nature, I looked up the history of that year, and here are some of its big events:

• James Monroe's daughter, Maria, got married in the White House.

- Missouri imposes a $1 "bachelor tax" on unmarried men from age 21 to 50.[24]
- U.S. Navy Captain Nathaniel Palmer discovered Antarctica.
- The tomato was proven to be not poisonous.

At this point, I'm thinking that we might need an economic theory based on spaghetti and penguins, but thankfully others have given the matter more thought. Angus Maddison himself attributes this long-term economic growth to three separate processes.[25] During the last millennium, settlers expanded into territories with fertile land and new biological resources. For example, Europeans' expansion into the Americas brought them crops such as corn, potatoes, sweet potatoes, and the "hey, it's not poisonous!" tomatoes. In addition, international trade increased with trade routes opening between Europe and China via caravans, and Africa and the Far East via ships. Also, the 1800s were a time of great technological innovation, including the industrial revolution, which created substantial wealth.

Poverty

Another way of thinking about income is to cast it in terms of poverty and examine how many people do not have "enough" money. The very concept of poverty, however, raises a philosophical question: Is poverty relative or absolute? A relative definition of poverty compares a person's income to others' in society—the person is poor if they have a lot less than other people, regardless of the actual amounts. Advantageously, relative measures of poverty allow for income expectations to change across time and place. We become keenly aware of the relative nature of poverty when we travel to poorer countries. When I was in college, I spent summers in Kenya and Honduras on short-term missions trips, and these experiences helped me to realize how remarkably wealthy my middle-class

---

Christians Making a Difference

Sometimes businesspeople are cast as the cause of poverty, but in 1994, a group of Christian businesspeople asked how they could be part of the solution. They formed Partners Worldwide, a nonprofit Christian organization that seeks to eliminate poverty through job creation. The key to their approach is to form partnerships with businesspeople in developing countries. Through these partnerships, Partners Worldwide provides mentoring, networking, training, and capital. They focus on the often-ignored small- and medium-sized businesses. One such partner is Bennie Brown, a businesswoman in Ghana. She received business training from Partners Worldwide in which she learned not only to run a business but also to serve the people who worked for her. Armed with this knowledge, she founded Total Image, a clothes-making company, and she employs five people—people who can now make a living for themselves. In the last two years, Partners Worldwide has helped create or retain over 23,000 jobs in over twenty countries.[26]

---

family was. I've had friends who have moved to poor countries, and with their average American salaries, they are able to live like rich people—with servants and all the best things.

An absolute definition of poverty, in contrast, assumes that there is some level of income needed to meet basic material needs, and people are poor if they fall below that line. The official federal poverty line in the United States was developed by the Social Security Administration in the early 1960s.[27] They estimated how much it cost to have a minimally adequate diet, and they multiplied this number by 3 (their guess as to how much everything else would cost).[28] The poverty line is adjusted for family size and inflation. In 2009, the poverty level in the continental United States was $10,830 for one person, $14,570 for a family of two, $18,310 for three, $22,050 for four, and so on.

This absolute line-in-the-sand official poverty line allows us to track changes over time and compare different groups, but it's still arbitrary. A family of four isn't going to throw a party to celebrate that they've escaped poverty when they earn $22,051 in a year, and are hence officially over the poverty line. Some people above the poverty line think of themselves as poor, and some below it do not. Furthermore, it's not entirely clear that this official standard of poverty is correctly constructed. It uses pretax income, so it doesn't account for what poor people pay in taxes. It also doesn't include noncash benefits such as public housing, Medicaid, or food stamps.[29] It doesn't measure wealth, so conceivably you could be officially poor while having a lot of money in the bank.[30] Also, the cost of living relative to the cost of food can change over time.[31] Nonetheless, this official definition of poverty is probably the most widely used definition, so I will use it here.

To start with, being "poor" in America doesn't always fit our preconceptions. Many Americans understand poverty to mean living in homelessness and not knowing where your next meal will come from. Certainly some of the poor fit this description, but others have more means. On average, people below the poverty line spend $1.75 for every $1 of their formal income (due to income from noncash benefits, the informal economy, and gifts), so they have more money than is implied by the official poverty line. Also, more than 95% of them have a color television and a VCR or DVD player. About three-fourths have air-conditioning and own a microwave and a car or truck.[32] Forty percent own a home.[33] In fact, if we were to use a relative understanding of poverty, many "poor" Americans would fall into the middle class or even well-to-do in poorer countries.

Another misconception regards the permanency of poverty. While some Americans struggle in long-term, chronic poverty, for many others it's only a short-term experience. For example, a person starting a business may earn very little the first few years, even if they eventually become a success. Officially, they are poor those first years. A retiree can have considerable financial assets but relatively little income. A graduate student can earn small stipends while launching their career. In fact, my wife and I were in graduate school when we had our first child, and we qualified for low-income food programs. While we appreciated this program, we never thought of ourselves as poor. A study in the early 1990s illustrates the often-episodic nature of poverty. In 1993 and 1994, 30% of Americans were below the poverty line for at least two consecutive months, but only 5% were below it for all two years.[34]

With these qualifications in mind, how many Americans are officially poor? As of 2008, it was 13.2%. Figure 3.3 plots the poverty rate over the past fifty years, and it breaks into two distinct time periods. From 1959 through 1973, the U.S. poverty rate dropped by half, from 22.4% to a historic low of 11.1%. Since 1973, however, it has bounced around between 11% and 15%.[35] Economist Robert Plotnick has applied today's definition of poverty to even earlier in the century, and he found that from 1915 to 1940, between 50% and 75% of Americans lived in poverty.[36] So over the last century, the poverty rate dropped substantially through 1973, after which it has leveled off.

Within this general trend in poverty, different groups in society have had different experiences. Notably, the relationship between age and poverty has changed considerably. As shown in Figure 3.3, poverty among people over age sixty-five has steadily dropped. In 1973 it was 16%, and now it's about 10%. In contrast, poverty among children has become more widespread. In 1973, 14% of children under age eighteen lived in poverty, and now it's up to 19%. Poverty among the aged has dropped because of the safety net provided by inflation-adjusted social security benefits.[37] Among children it increased in part due to there being more single-parent families, who tend to be poorer than two-parent families.[38]

Poverty also varies widely across race and ethnic groups. Whites and Asians have relatively low poverty rates, at 8.6% and 11.8% respectively; in contrast, African-Americans and Hispanics are at 24.7% and 23.2%. As such, black families are about three times more likely to be poor than white families. The good news is that

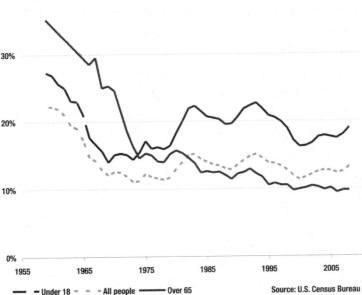

Figure 3.3: U.S. Poverty Rates, by Age

— ─ Under 18   ─ ─ ─ All people   ━━━ Over 65   Source: U.S. Census Bureau

poverty has declined substantially among African-Americans. In 1959, over half (55%) of black families lived in poverty, more than double what it is now.

Many other factors are associated with poverty. Employment, obviously, mitigates poverty. Among full-time, year-round workers, only about 3% are officially poor.[39] Poverty rates are highest in the South and lower Midwest. Looking at a map of American poverty rates, it appears that poverty is lowest where you have to shovel snow in the winter or are within a few hours of the ocean. Political scientist James Q. Wilson summarized poverty's association with several demographic characteristics when he observed that a person can mostly avoid poverty by doing three things: finish high school, marry before having a child, and not have children before age twenty. Families that do not fit these criteria have poverty rates at about 75%.[40]

When we look at poverty in the world, we can't use America's definition of poverty because so many other countries have substantially lower incomes than we do. Instead, measures of worldwide poverty are set much lower. A commonly used yet heart-wrenching measure defines extreme poverty as living on less than $1.25 a day.[41] Figure 3.4 plots extreme poverty levels for developing countries as well as several poorer regions. In 1981, a full 52% of people living in developing countries lived in extreme poverty, and this has fallen to 26% in 2005—a full 50% reduction in only twenty-five years.[42] The United Nations estimates that global poverty declined more in the last fifty years than it did in the previous five hundred years![43]

This decline in extreme poverty did not occur everywhere in the developing world; in fact, most of it happened in East and South Asia. As shown in Figure 3.4, East Asia, which includes China, had a mind-boggling 79% rate of extreme poverty in 1981, and

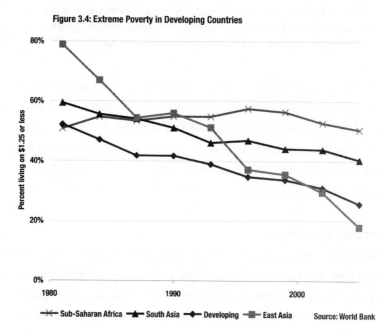

Figure 3.4: Extreme Poverty in Developing Countries

Source: World Bank

Christians Making a Difference

In the late 1990s, Jeff Rutt, a home builder in Lancaster, Pennsylvania, participated in church mission trips to deliver food, clothing, and medical supplies to an impoverished city in Ukraine. On one of these trips, a local pastor pulled Jeff aside and told him that the delivered supplies weren't actually helping because local businesses couldn't compete with them and the fostered dependence. Jeff returned home determined to find a solution, and his research led him to the idea of microfinance. With microfinance, a small loan is given to entrepreneurs in developing countries, and with this loan the entrepreneurs start or expand their businesses. This, in turn, provides more income for them, which they use for better food, housing, and education for their children. Microfinance is a long-term solution that gives people a strong sense of pride in their work.

Armed with this approach, Jeff founded HOPE International, a Christian-based ministry that seeks to free the world's poor from their poverty. HOPE International provides loans between $50 and $2,000, and these loans finance business such as food preparation, animal husbandry, sewing, painting, vending, basket weaving, and car repair. Over 99% of the borrowers pay their loan back in full, giving HOPE resources to invest in others. HOPE works in over a dozen of the world's most needy countries, including Afghanistan, Congo, Burundi, Dominican Republic, Haiti, Romania, and Rwanda. Between their financing and other business programs, HOPE has reached nearly 250,000 entrepreneurs around the world.[44]

---

this dropped all the way down to 18% by 2005—an extraordinary, and perhaps unprecedented, economic transformation. South Asia, which includes India, also had its poverty rate drop, from 42% to 24% between 1981 and 2005. Sub-Saharan Africa, unfortunately, has not enjoyed the same success. Its extreme poverty levels have remained mostly stable in recent decades, ranging between 50% and 58%.

Income Inequality

Ideas of income and poverty are pretty easy to understand, but now we'll look at a financial measure that's a little less straightforward. Income inequality regards the distribution of income throughout society, and it compares how poor the poor are compared to how rich the rich are. Imagine two societies. In one society every single person makes $50,000 a year, and in the second society one-third make $20,000, one-third make $50,000, and one-third make $80,000. Both societies' average income level is $50,000, but the second society has more income inequality, for there is a greater distance between the poor and the rich.

Here's something to mull over: Should we care about income inequality? For example, is someone making $50,000 in a low-inequality society better off than someone making the same amount in a high-inequality society? The research literature isn't entirely clear on this point. Some studies have linked income inequality to civic alienation, discontentment, and low rates of economic growth.[45] Others have concluded that income inequality has uncertain effects.[46] Income inequality may be negative or neutral, but there isn't much reason to think that it's a positive feature for societies.[47] Basically, it's a philosophical question of fairness. Is it right for some people to have so much when others have so little?

Economists measure income inequality in various ways, but for this section I'll use what I see as the most intuitive measure—how much money people earn in different strata of society. Economists often divide American households by income into five different categories—from the top-earning 20% down to the bottom 20%. If we measure the average income level of these categories from 1967 to 2008,[48] we find that average income levels actually increased for all five income groups. For Americans living in the bottom fifth of income, it increased by 29%, from an average of about $9,000 in 1967 to about $11,700 in 2008. (Note: Dollar amounts are adjusted for inflation.) For the second fifth it increased 18%, and for the middle fifth it increased 26%. The fourth group, what would roughly correspond to the middle class, increased more, at 42%, and the wealthiest fifth of Americans increased at the highest rate of all—70%. Perhaps you've heard the expression that the "rich get richer and the poor get poorer." At least since 1967, it would be truer to say that the rich have gotten a lot richer and the poor only somewhat richer.[49] As a result, income inequality has grown.

Over the span of the twentieth century, income inequality fell and then rose again. Income inequality was very high in the 1920s— even higher than it is now. From there, inequality dropped steadily through the 1950s, and from the mid-1950s through about 1970, inequality levels were at their lowest, after which they started rising to the present day.[50] To illustrate this general pattern of inequality, in 1932 the top 10% of American households earned 47% of all income in the country. By 1967, this had dropped down to 33%, and by the mid-1990s it had risen again to above 40%.[51]

There is an important qualification to these data, however. It turns out that wealthier households have more people living in them than do poorer households. The top-earning fifth of households have 64 million people living in them compared to only 39 million in the bottom fifth.[52] Wealthier households often have multiple-income earners (thus making them wealthier). The poorest households include many retired people and single-parent families, making them both smaller and poorer. As a consequence, the data presented above reflect a disproportionate number of people among the well-to-do families.

Why has income inequality grown in recent decades? Scholars have hotly debated this issue and point to various reasons. Many high-paying, secure manufacturing jobs have been lost.[53] The influence of labor unions has declined.[54] Illegal immigration has brought many people to the country who tend to start at lower wages.[55] Inflation has eroded the real value of the minimum wage.[56] High-earning people are more likely to marry one another than in the past.[57] Incomes have risen most for workers with a college education and strong technical skills.[58]

Now I would like to describe income inequality worldwide,

and this requires telling you about a unique economic statistic. Way back when, a group of economists shut their office doors, put on their best tweed sports coats, read from ancient texts, and created a statistic that measures economic inequality. How exactly is it calculated? They won't tell us—only that it ranges from 0 (absolute equality) to 100 (absolute inequality). The higher a country's score, the more inequality it has. Thankfully, though, they gave it an easy-to-pronounce name: the Gini index (as in a "genie" in a bottle).[59]

Armed with the Gini index, we can compare countries worldwide.[60] The countries with the least inequality (i.e., Gini scores below 30) tend to be wealthy countries, primarily in Europe. They include Norway, Sweden, Japan, Finland, Austria, Denmark, Germany, Czech Republic, Slovakia, Croatia, Bulgaria, Belarus, Ukraine, and Ethiopia. The countries with the most inequality (i.e., Gini scores over 55) tend to be in Sub-Saharan Africa or Latin America, and they include Brazil, Columbia, Honduras, Bolivia, Botswana, Namibia, Comoros, Angola, and Haiti.

Where does the United States fit in? It has a Gini score of 40.8, which puts it right in the middle. It ranks 73 out of 142 countries, based on data from the World Bank. Among wealthy countries, however, the U.S. has a relatively high level of inequality. Of the twenty-five richest countries in the world, the United States has the third highest level of inequality. Only Singapore and Hong Kong are wealthy countries with more inequality. This suggests that, overall, we Americans could distribute income more fairly.

Unemployment

Another aspect of economic life is employment, which provides most of us with most of our money. Those people not able to find employment usually face significant hardships. Unemployment is officially defined as not having a job, having actively looked for work in the past four weeks and being available for work, or having

---

Christians Making a Difference

Urban Ministry is a ministry of the United Methodist Church in Birmingham, Alabama. Their mission is to bring compassion and wholeness to the urban poor in Birmingham—some of the poorest people in the country. Urban Ministry accomplishes this mission both by alleviating the immediate suffering of the poor and working to end the long-term causes of poverty in Birmingham. They have many different programs, including:
- a community kitchen, which feeds a hot lunch to the poor;
- a food pantry to provide nonperishable food to people in need;
- a kids' program in which kids can come after school and play, sing, draw, and learn;
- an assistance ministry that helps pay the rent and utilities for families in crisis;
- a prison ministry in which they visit and counsel men on death row.

Countless thousands of the poor and needy have had their lives made better through the Urban Ministry.[61]

---

been laid off from a job and expecting to be called back.[62] Figure 3.5 plots U.S. unemployment rates since 1900 (for civilians who are sixteen or older).[63] As you can see, unemployment is cyclical. Over the past century it has bounced between 1% and 10% with one major exception: the Great Depression. Unemployment peaked at over 25% in 1933, and it stayed very high through the start of World War II. In recent years, the nation went through another recession. Figure 3.5 highlights the severity of it, for it was one of only three times in the past century (other than the Great Depression) when the unemployment rate approached 10%. When unemployment does increase, it hits blue-collar workers harder than those without college degrees.[64]

The nature of unemployment has changed over the last century. In the early 1900s, many Americans did seasonal work, which meant that they had periodic episodes of unemployment lasting weeks or maybe a few months. Starting with Henry Ford's assembly lines in the 1920s, more people had the same job for life, and the work force divided between the steadily employed and the

Figure 3.5: U.S. Unemployment Rates Since 1900

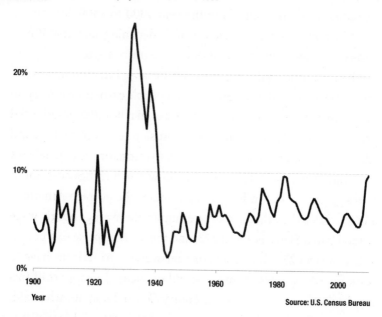

Source: U.S. Census Bureau

unemployed.[65] Compared to a century ago, we now have fewer workers who experience unemployment, but those who do, remain so for much longer.[66]

What Things Cost

This chapter so far has focused on how much money people get, but that's only half of the equation. The other half is how much things cost, because what good is having more money if the price of things gets even higher? Because of inflation, the price in dollars of just about everything is higher than it used to be, but how has the real cost (i.e., adjusted for inflation) of what we buy changed?

Many Americans think that life was cheaper in the good ol' days, but this ignores the effect of inflation. In actual fact, the real prices of most things have dropped over time as people have become more efficient at producing and distributing goods and services.[67]

As a simple example, the inflation-adjusted price of grain in Europe remained roughly stable from the year 1300 to 1800. Starting in 1800, however, its price started steadily declining such that it now costs only one-tenth of what it did two centuries ago.[68]

It gets a little confusing, however, because inflation means not only that things cost more but also that people earn more money, so the relative cost of an item can decrease even if its inflation-adjusted price increases. To overcome this confusion, economists Cox and Alm have popularized a new approach to estimating the "true" cost of things over time.[69] They estimate how much things cost not in terms of dollars but in how many minutes the average American had to work to buy that item. For example, the average hourly wage in the United States is about $23, and the average price of a pound of bacon is $3.25. This means that on average, Americans have to work for 8.5 minutes to buy a pound of bacon. In support of this approach, Cox and Alm quote Henry David Thoreau, who said, "The cost of a thing is the amount of what I will call life which is required to be exchanged for it, immediately and in the long run."[70]

Minutes-worked gives us a useful way to examine the cost of living over time. And guess what: Just about everything is cheaper now. Figure 3.6 reports the cost in minutes-worked of various items since 1920. A loaf of bread cost 13 minutes of work in 1920, and now it costs 3.5 minutes. A gallon of milk dropped from 37 minutes to 7 minutes. A 3-pound chicken dropped from 147 minutes to 14 minutes. Chocolate, oranges, electricity, and even Levi's have dropped in price over the last 90 years.[71] A Big Mac cost about 30 minutes of work in the 1950s; now it's about 3 minutes.[72] An even greater drop occurred with long-distance phone calls. A 3-minute coast-to-coast call cost 1,800 minutes in 1920, but now it's only 2 minutes. This change resonates with me because when I was a kid, long-distance calls were a big deal. We would talk to our grandparents only on holidays and special occasions, and the whole family would stand excitedly in the kitchen, each taking a one-minute, carefully timed turn. Now I don't even consider the cost of calls when I make them. One thing that has gotten slightly more expensive is movie tickets. In 1920 they cost 17 minutes of work, and now they cost 19 minutes.

Figure 3.6: The Cost of Various Goods in Minutes Worked

	1920	1940	1960	1980	1998
Hershey's chocolate bar	6	5	1.3	2	2.1
Loaf of bread (1 lb)	13	7	5.4	4	3.5
Movie ticket	17	16	17	22	19
Gallon of gas	32	17	8.3	10	5.7
Milk	37	21	13	8.7	7
Dozen oranges	69	27	20	11	9
3-pound chicken	147	74	33	18	14
Pair of Levi's	636	270	156	168	204
Electricity (100 hours)	816	352	69	45	38
3-minute phone call coast-to-coast	1803	367	60	11	2

Cells report minutes worked for median income required to purchase an item
(Source: Cox and Alm, 1999, 43)

Using this approach, we can go back even further. Suppose that you lived in France and you wanted to travel from Paris to Bordeaux. In the late 1800s, this trip would have cost a month's worth of a clerk's wages, but now it costs only about a day's worth, and, as a bonus, the trip is fifty times as fast.[73]

Not only are things cheaper now, but many of them are better in quality.[74] When I was growing up, the common wisdom was that a well-maintained car would make it to 100,000 miles. Now cars last much longer. Our day-to-day car just flipped 200,000 miles. Similarly, prescription drugs today treat a wider range of ailments more effectively than they used to. We can also buy stuff that wasn't even available in past decades, including microwave ovens, cell phones, soft contact lenses, camcorders, and computers.[75] The crowning example of how much we have available? Supermarkets. Super-markets sell thousands and thousands of items, and their food is fresh and safe.[76] Kings and queens of the past lived their whole lives without seeing a fraction of what is available to us down the street.

Unfortunately, not everything in life is cheaper now. Two things that have gotten more expensive are higher education and medicine. Since the mid–1960s, college tuition at public universities has more than doubled in terms of work-hours, and it has increased even more at private universities.[77] Likewise, the cost of medical care has soared over the past decades, though health insurance covers many health costs (for those who have it).[78] For example, in 2001 a family of four in the U.S. spent about $15,000 a year for health-care costs, but only $4,000 of this was out-of-pocket.[79] It's difficult to accurately measure the increased cost of medical care, though, because the quality of the care has steadily increased with advances in medical technology and drugs, so we're getting more for our money.

What about housing? Here the story is mixed. In terms of real dollars, the median price of a new house has gone up in past decades. The median price of existing family homes has increased in the last generation from $142,000 to $223,000 (in inflation-adjusted dollars).[80] Counteracting the higher price tag, though, is that people make more money now and mortgage rates are lower, so the actual number of hours needed to pay for a house is about the same now as it was in the 1970s.[81] In addition, new single-family houses are about 50% bigger now, meaning that people are often getting more house for the money. The real change in housing, though, has been in ownership rates. In 1900, a little over one-third of Americans owned their homes, and now it's about two-thirds.[82]

It's difficult to compare the cost of living worldwide because the nature of goods and services varies widely by location. A median-priced house in the United States, for example, is very different from one in Sub-Saharan Africa. At this point we are saved by Ronald

McDonald. By international law, all Big Macs have to have two whole-beef patties, special sauce, lettuce, cheese, pickles, and onions on a sesame seed bun.[83] This allows us to compare the price of Big Macs around the world. This "Big Mac Index" was created by *The Economist* magazine, and it provides a rough guide to the relative purchasing power worldwide.[84] The most expensive Big Macs are found in Norway, Sweden, and Switzerland, where they cost more than $6 each. The cheapest are in the Ukraine, Sri Lanka, Hong Kong, and China, where they cost less than $2. If we factor in average wage rates, Americans have to work, on average, about 12 minutes to buy a Big Mac. (And that's time well-spent!) In contrast, an average worker in Nairobi, Kenya, has to work 158 minutes, and one in Mexico City works 129 minutes.[85] This highlights how much more people in poorer countries have to work just to buy the basics of life (like a Big Mac).

Savings and Debt

I conclude this chapter with something near and dear to my heart: Saving too little money and owing too much. Americans are good at many things, but saving money is not one of them. Figure 3.7 plots Americans' personal savings rates since 1959.[86] This is calculated by starting with disposable, after-tax income and subtracting personal spending on things like food, housing, transportation, and entertainment. What's left is termed *savings*. From the 1960s through the mid-1980s, Americans usually saved about 8% to 10% of their income. Starting in the mid-1980s, our savings rates started dropping such that by 2005, we were barely saving 2% (though it has since risen to 5%).

Why can't Johnny save money? In the 1980s and 1990s, many Americans saw the value of their houses rise substantially, and they treated the value of their house as a savings account, one easily accessed with a home equity loan. Also, people save less money

Figure 3.7: Americans' Savings Rate and Debt Ratio

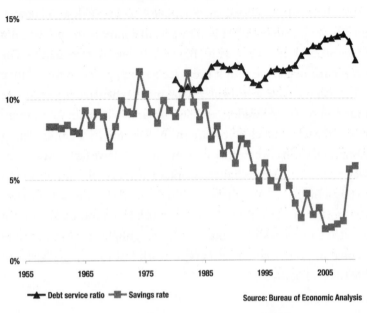

▲ Debt service ratio ■ Savings rate   Source: Bureau of Economic Analysis

when they expect their future earnings to rise. This happened more in past decades. Generally speaking, savings rates increase during bad times. This is seen in Figure 3.7 with the economic recessions in the early 1970s, early 1980s, and in 2008.[87]

Coupled with our decreased savings is our increased borrowing.[88] Why save money for college, a house, or retirement when we can borrow it? Borrowing money has become much easier in recent years. To illustrate, when I graduated from high school in 1980, it took some work to get credit cards. I started with the lowly Sears charge card, which I used for several months, carefully paying it off each month. This allowed me to take the next step: gasoline and other department store cards. Finally, with my fledgling credit history, I obtained the Holy Grail of consumer spending: a Visa card! In contrast, banks today actively recruit borrowers, and they seem ready to give credit cards to just about anyone—even dogs and children.[89]

One way of measuring debt is called household debt service ratio. This is how much money people spend of their personal, disposable income to cover the interest on mortgages and consumer debt.[90] Americans' debt service ratio is not a pretty sight. In the early 1980s, Americans paid about 11% of their incomes to mortgage and debt. By 2008, this increased to nearly 14% before dropping in the past two recessionary years. In 1983, Americans owed about 43% of their average, annual incomes, and now we owe more than a year's worth of work.[91]

Overall, how has the U.S. and the world been doing financially? In the long term, very good. Personal incomes have risen steadily, poverty is in decline, and the prices of most goods have gone down. Of course, the picture is not perfect. There is always room for improvement, but it's good to keep in mind that we have much to be thankful for (and then pay off our credit cards).

CHAPTER 4

ARE WE DUMBER THAN WE USED TO BE?

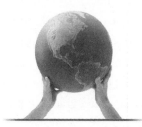

No reliable evidence exists that students as a whole are perform-
ing less well than they did 25 years ago.
—*Derek Bok, former president of
Harvard*[1]

It's odd that a narrative of crisis, of a systematic failure, in
American education is currently so pervasive.
—*Nicholas Lemann,* The New Yorker[2]

The current generation has made massive gains on all kinds of
IQ tests.
—*James Flynn, political scientist*[3]

Education

It's hard to get people on the left and right to agree about much of
anything, but there is one point that you'll hear from both sides:
Our schools are in bad shape. From the rooftops people shout that
we're falling behind globally in all areas of education, to the point

that soon Americans won't be able to compete on the job market. If only we could get back to the glory days of American education, back to when we knew how to read, write, and do math.

But is this true? Have we really lost our ability to teach our children?

Let's start with how much education children receive today as compared to previous generations. As you've probably heard by now, people who go to school make more money. The median income for high school dropouts is $19,000; for high school graduates $27,000; for college graduates $47,000; and for those with advanced degrees $60,000.[4] Not that you get an automatic pay raise when you finish your degree. Nor is there a $20,000 check tucked into your diploma. The degree itself isn't the only cause of these income differences. After all, a person with a college degree might not do well in the workplace, and a person with a graduate degree might have done just fine even without the extra education. Nonetheless, the level of education usually correlates to a better job, not only in terms of income, but also health insurance, job autonomy, and other things we're looking for.[5]

Over the past century, Americans' education levels have gone up, up, and then up some more. Figure 4.1 plots changes in American educational attainment since 1910 at three different levels: How many American adults (over age twenty-five) attended less than five years of elementary school, how many completed four years of high school, and how many finished four years of college.[6] A century ago, about three-quarters of American adults had only a fifth-grade education; 14% had four years of high school; and only about 3% had four years of college. Since then, education levels have steadily increased such that now 85% of American adults have four years of high school and 27% have at least four years of college. (And nearly every adult has gotten past the fifth grade.)

In terms of how many years Americans spend in school, in 1910,

Figure 4.1: Educational Attainment

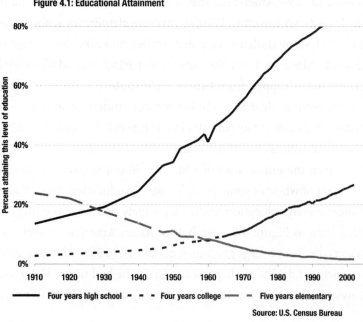

Source: U.S. Census Bureau

thirty-year-old adults averaged eight years of schooling. This rose sharply to thirteen years by 1970, and it has continued to increase ever since, though at a slower rate. Currently, Americans average about fourteen years in school.[7] Since the 1960s, school enrollment rates for kids ages 8 to 15 have been at nearly 100%. Years of schooling has increased because more families are sending their kids to preschool. Also, students are staying in school longer, often into their twenties.[8] My wife and I have done our share to contribute to this latter trend. When giving information for my youngest son's birth certificate, we were asked how many years of education we had. It took a few moments of thought, but we sheepishly admitted that we had fifty-two years of education between us, K through PhD.[9] (And, yes, we're still paying off our student loans as our oldest is getting ready for college.)

Here's something that may shock you: Despite the fact that

more and more Americans attend school, class sizes have actually decreased over time.[10] In 1910, the average elementary school class had thirty-four students for every teacher, and now the average is down to nineteen. Over the same time period, secondary-school classes have dropped from twenty-eight students to fifteen. While it's not entirely clear that a lower teacher-student ratio results in better education, many educators view it as helpful, and, if nothing else, it contributes to a more manageable classroom.

Given the importance of education in our society, we should be aware of whether some groups have less education than others. Unfortunately, education levels vary widely by race and ethnicity. As shown in Figure 4.2, over half of Asian-Americans (over age twenty-five) are college graduates, compared to 30% of whites, 20% of blacks, and 13% of Hispanics.[11] That's the bad news. The good news is that education levels are increasing for all four of these

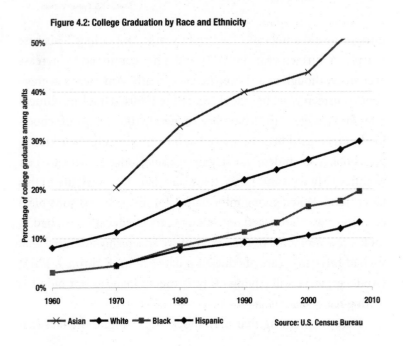

Figure 4.2: College Graduation by Race and Ethnicity

groups. Over the last forty years, the percentage of Asian, white, and Hispanic college graduates has more than doubled, and the percentage of African-Americans more than quadrupled—a legacy of the civil rights movement.[12]

Education levels have risen not only in the United States, but also worldwide, though at different times for different countries. This is shown in Figure 4.3, which plots education levels over the past two centuries for the U.S., France, Germany, the United Kingdom, Japan, China, and India.[13] Education levels in the first five countries have risen steadily for two centuries. For example, Japan averaged less than two years of education in 1870, but it's up to more than fourteen years now. China and India, in contrast, started much later. They averaged less than two years of education in 1950, and now, just forty years later, China averages more than eight years of education and India more than five.

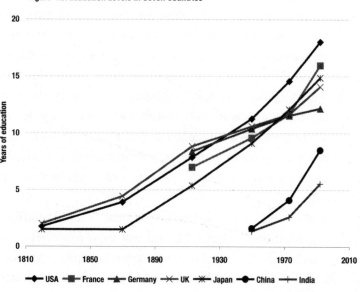

Figure 4.3: Education Levels in Seven Countries

Source: Maddison

Education levels have risen even in less-developed countries. In just the six years between 1999 and 2005, the percentage of primary-aged children worldwide enrolled in school rose from 83% to 87%, and the number of children not in school dropped from 96 million to 74 million. This increase was especially pronounced in some of the poorest regions of the world, including Sub-Saharan Africa, which saw a 23% increase in primary-school enrollment.[14] Many regions of the world have universal primary education, meaning that more than 90% of the primary-school-age children are in school. These include North America, Europe, East Asia, Latin America, and the Caribbean. The Arab States and Central, South, and West Asia have enrollment rates between 80% and 90%, and countries in Sub-Saharan Africa have enrollment rates below 80%.[15] In less-developed countries, as would be expected, the least educated children are often those from poorer or indigenous populations. Also, children in rural settings are less educated because of their greater distance from urban education centers and frequent social marginalization.[16]

Gender differences in education worldwide are a bit complex because they vary by both the development level of a country as well as the particular stage of education. In more developed countries, like the United States, nearly all school-age children attend school, so there is little gender disparity in primary or secondary education enrollment. In higher education, however, more women go to college than do men, a trend of the last several decades. In contrast, in less-developed countries, primary education is not always available for all children, and when it isn't, boys are more likely to be sent to school than girls.

A study by the United Nations Educational, Scientific and Cultural Organization (UNESCO) found that most countries (118) worldwide had gender equality in primary schooling.[17] Sixty-four countries had significantly more boys in their primary schools, and only six countries had more girls. The pattern is mixed with

---

Christians Making a Difference

Berea College is a nondenominational Christian college in Kentucky. It has a rich history, being the first racially integrated college in the South, and it is one of the nation's highest-ranked liberal arts colleges (number 68 in a recent ranking). What's most distinctive about it, however, is that it's free. That's right. Berea College charges no tuition to any student; instead, students are required to work on campus for at least ten hours a week. In exchange, all students are given a full four-year scholarship worth over $100,000. This provides a college education for children from low-income families throughout Appalachia and the country.[18]

---

secondary education, with about an equal number of countries (61) having more boys in secondary education as countries having more girls in them (53). At the college level, however, women enjoy a distinct advantage worldwide. In 48 countries, men are disproportionately represented in colleges, but in nearly double that many, 92 countries, women are overrepresented.

This gendered pattern of education happens, in part, because in many cultures, boys and young men are expected to provide for their families, and so they quit schooling to find work. For example, in Lesotho, Africa, boys commonly drop out of school to start herding livestock, making them into responsible members of their families. Likewise, in Chile, poor boys are four times more likely than girls to quit school and enter the labor market.[19]

Literacy

Just because the years of education have gone up around the globe, does that mean that kids are, in fact, learning more? At a very basic level, we can look at literacy rates to answer this question. Most Americans are literate, reflecting remarkable progress over the last century. As shown in Figure 4.4, in 1870, only 80% of the general population (including 20% of blacks and other non-whites) could read and write.[20] These numbers rapidly increased in the following decades, so that by

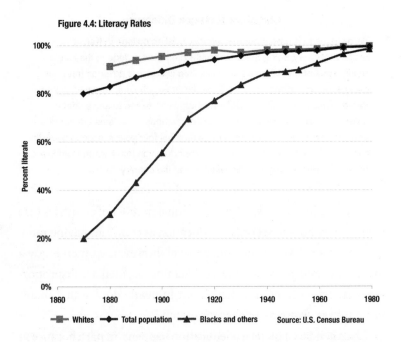

Figure 4.4: Literacy Rates

Whites Total population Blacks and others Source: U.S. Census Bureau

the eve of World War II, 97% of the population (and 89% of African-Americans) were literate. By the year 1979, more than 98% of both whites and blacks were literate. That's a social triumph.

Worldwide, an estimated 82% of all people can read and write. But unfortunately, illiteracy is still a problem in some parts of the world. South and West Asia as well as Sub-Saharan Africa have the lowest literacy rates—below 60% as of 2004. India alone, with its large population, has over one-third of all illiterate adults in the world.[21] The Arab states and the Caribbean countries have about 70% literacy.[22] Illiteracy rates in developing countries are highest for women, who account for 64% of all adult illiteracy. This is no surprise given the lower rates of primary education among girls in developing countries.

But the good news is that illiteracy has steadily dropped world-wide. Just a century ago, in 1915, only about 1 in 4 adults worldwide

Christians Making a Difference

My wife and I taught our two sons to read, and I thought that was pretty cool, but William Kofmehl Jr. and his wife, Linda, have taught tens of thousands of people to read. In 1975, they founded Christian Literacy Associates with the vision of combating illiteracy in and around Pittsburgh, Pennsylvania. Dr. Kofmehl, who received his PhD in education, developed the Christian Literacy Series, a basic reading textbook that uses biblical content. With this and other materials, the Christian Literacy Associates have trained over five thousand local volunteers as reading tutors, and over 20,000 people in the Pittsburgh area have participated in their programs. Furthermore, partnering with various global relief organizations, such as World Vision, they have taught 70,000 people to read in some of the world's poorest countries, such as Malawi and Haiti. Many of these recipients were girls and women who might otherwise not receive this essential component of a proper education.[23]

could read and write.[24] By 1970, global adult literacy reached 47%, on its way to its current level of 82%.[25] Global literacy has risen for various reasons, including modern economic growth and expanded educational opportunities. But another reason traces back to the Protestant Reformation. Martin Luther taught a gospel of personal salvation, emphasizing the need for people to read the Bible for themselves. This meant they needed to be able to read, so for many years Christian churches have taken up the mission of educating young people.[26]

Intelligence

Adding to education and literacy is the topic of intelligence. This is tricky to analyze because it's a broad topic that's difficult to even define. Furthermore, we don't even know if there's only one type of intelligence or many. American psychologist Howard Gardner identified eight types of intelligence, including logical, linguistic, musical, emotional, spatial, and interpersonal.[27] Given these ambiguities, there's no conclusive way to track intelligence; however, available evidence suggests that overall, people may be getting smarter.

One imperfect measure of intelligence is standardized test scores. In the past decade, the role of the SAT and other standardized tests has become controversial. It's likely that these tests capture only some types of intelligence but miss other forms. Also, while they are correlated with future academic achievement, the correlation is far from perfect, and many argue that standardized testing has become too important in education—leading teachers to "teach for the test" rather than being focused on fuller educational development.[28]

Keeping these caveats in mind, how have test scores changed in recent decades? Since the early 1970s, the U.S. Department of Education has regularly tested the reading and math skills of thousands of school kids ages 9, 13, and 17. Figure 4.5 plots how these age groups have fared over the last four decades.[29] With reading, the average scores of 9-year-olds increased somewhat and for 13-year-olds they increased slightly. The scores of 17-year-olds, however, have remained virtually unchanged. With math, the scores of 9-year-olds increased substantially, 13-year-olds somewhat, and 17-year-olds stayed about the same.

More students are also taking advanced mathematics classes. In 1986, only 35% of 13-year-olds took algebra or pre-algebra, but this number climbed to 62% by 2008.[30] I know that my son in high school has already taken more advanced math classes than I took in college. So we have good news for younger kids, and 17-year-olds are at least not getting worse. (T-shirt idea for high school kids: "No dumber than you were.")

A similar story emerges with college entrance tests.[31] SAT scores for critical reading dropped from 1975 to 1980, but they have remained roughly stable since. Math scores have increased substantially since 1975. The same holds true with the ACT. ACT English scores have remained stable since 1990, but math scores have risen steadily. Granted, these college-entrance exams are more

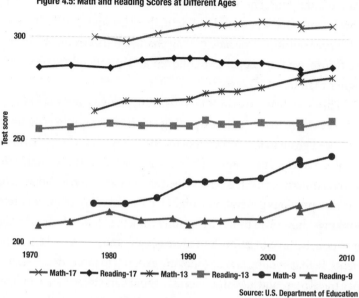

Figure 4.5: Math and Reading Scores at Different Ages

Source: U.S. Department of Education

difficult to interpret because they are optional and students can retake them. Nonetheless, they do conform to the patterns found in other standardized tests.[32]

Examining intelligence trends brings us to a fascinating story centered on a New Zealand psychologist named James Flynn. He was your run-of-the-mill island-based research psychologist until 1984, when he asked for and received the results of IQ tests given to two generations of eighteen-year-olds in Holland.[33] As Flynn examined the data, he found that Dutch teens in the 1980s scored substantially higher on the IQ tests than did their predecessors in the 1950s. This stoked his curiosity, so he started gathering IQ test results from around the world, including Europe, North America, Asia, and the developing world. Eventually he had data from thirty different countries, and in every case he found the same increase in IQ scores—about three points per decade. This rise in IQ scores was labeled the Flynn Effect. (Wouldn't it be great to have an effect named after you? The Wright Effect might be the startled look on a professor's face when students actually show up for office hours.)

Three points per decade is a big change. If this trend holds into the future, we can expect our children and grandchildren to score higher than us on IQ tests.

This worldwide rise in IQ scores is suggestive—but not conclusive—evidence that people are getting smarter. Various explanations have been given to it.[34] Some scholars, including Flynn himself, think that it results from the nature of IQ tests themselves. IQ tests emphasize abstract thinking, which is both valued and taught in today's society. In contrast, previous generations might have focused more on concrete thinking—how to do things well. Others link the Flynn Effect to better nutrition, better education, and increasingly complex social environments. Perhaps young people today are exposed to more ideas because they travel more and have more access to books and information online. Regardless of how we interpret the Flynn Effect, the overall evidence points to a better educated, more intelligent humanity.

What Have We Learned?

So what does all this mean? Surely we hear more bad news than good news when it comes to the state of education in our country and our world. Are we being lied to? Not necessarily. Going back to something I said in chapter 1, just because the trend is good—i.e., just because things are heading in the right direction—doesn't mean everything is as it should be. We must continue to evaluate what is working and what is not. Surely more can be done to level the playing field when it comes to national and global education. Nevertheless, we should be grateful to God that for most people in most of the world, education is heading in the right direction, and more and more children are getting opportunities to improve their lives.

CHAPTER 5

ARE WE SICKER THAN WE USED TO BE?

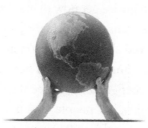

The doubling of life expectancy since the start of the industrial revolution is "the greatest miracle in the history of our species."
—New York Times *magazine*[1]

Your ancestors from four generations ago "would be dazzled. Unlimited food at affordable prices, never the slightest worry about shortage, unlimited variety—strawberries in March!"
—*Greg Easterbrook, writer*[2]

The world is, at last, making some real progress in its response to AIDS.
—*Joint United Nations Programme on HIV/AIDS*[3]

Cancer rates are on the rise. AIDS is a global scourge. Diabetes is becoming an epidemic. Children are starving everywhere. According to what we read in magazines and watch on TV, it seems unlikely we'll live past Friday, let alone until we're old enough to start getting checks from social security (which we're told will be bankrupt by then anyway—but that's a crisis for another day). But maybe we're not getting the full picture when it comes to our health. If we take a closer look at it, we may find that with this issue, there is rampant good news.

Life Expectancy

The single best measure of health is how long people live, for sick people tend to die more often than healthy people. The good news is that Americans are living longer now than ever, as we see in Figure 5.1, which plots Americans' life expectancy since the year 1900.[4] A baby born in 1900 lived about 47 years on average. A 1950s baby could expect 68 years, and a baby born now can expect about 78 years. Much of this change in life expectancy is due to lessening rates of infant mortality, but people who make it into adulthood also live longer. A 40-year-old in 1900 could expect to live to age 68. Nowadays, it's 80 years old. A 65-year-old in 1990 generally lived to age 77, and now it's 84.

When it comes to how long we live, there are both racial and gender differences. Racial differences, while still in existence, have lessened over time. An African-American born in 1900 lived to an average of only thirty-four years—sixteen years less than whites. Today the age-expectancy difference between the two races is only five years. In contrast, gender differences have actually increased slightly. A boy born in 1900 lived about three fewer years than a girl, but boys born today can expect to live five fewer years.[5] Women live longer than men due to various genetic and environmental reasons, including the facts that women are less likely to smoke cigarettes, they eat foods lower in cholesterol, and they deal with their stress more effectively.[6] (Also, men suffer from exposure to the elements while taking the trash out every week.)

We take our current long lives for granted, but think for a

Figure 5.1: Life Expectancy

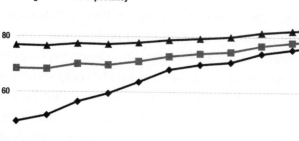
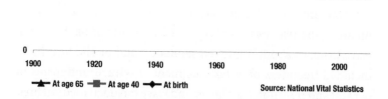

Source: National Vital Statistics

moment about what a change this is from previous generations. In 1890, usually one parent would not live long enough to see their children get married.[7] Now we live long enough to see our grand-children get married. Imagine high school reunions back then. The twentieth class reunion would have a lot of empty seats. My own mother passed away suddenly and unexpectedly when she was sixty-two years old. Besides feeling tremendous pain, I also had a sense of unfairness that she was taken from us so early; and yet a century ago, she would have been considered relatively long-lived.

Americans' longevity has many consequences, not the least of which is its effect on the social security system. The federal retire-ment age was initially set at 65 years, because a government study in 1928 estimated that life expectancy would eventually rise to 65 years. Lawmakers used this age, thinking that around half of Ameri-cans would pass away before reaching it, and social security would take care of the other, longer-lived half. Life expectancy did reach 65 years in the 1940s, but it kept going up. Now, 83% of children born are expected to live to age 65.[8] This poses a problem for the long-term viability of social security—we're living too long. This raises an interesting idea. The benefits paid by social security are pegged to inflation rates, so they go up every year. What if eligibility for it was pegged to life expectancy? If so, people would have to wait until age 78 to receive full social security benefits—much later than the current age of 67 (for people born in 1960 or later). I don't advocate this change, but it helps us to appreciate even more how much longer we are all living.

Why are Americans living longer? Three waves of life improvements in the twentieth century had a dramatic impact.[9] The first wave brought about improved sanitation and public health. This included treatment of water, treatment of sewage, and inspection of meat and milk quality. The second wave included medical breakthroughs against specific diseases and infections. For example, inoculations mostly eradicated smallpox, polio, and measles, and antibiotics such as penicillin helped cure pneumonia and other illnesses. The third wave brought medical developments that treated heart disease, cancer, and other ailments of middle-aged and elderly people.

Worldwide, life expectancy has been steadily rising for several centuries now. For much of human history, a newborn could be expected to live, on average, only 20 to 30 years. This number is derived from various data sources, including skeletal remains in North Africa and Roman burial records.[10] Likewise, financial records from fourteenth-century England put life expectancy at about 25 years. A study of Benedict monks in the 1400s found that novices entering the order at age 18 could expect to live, on average, another 10 years, to age 28.[11] A study of British Royalty in the seventeenth century found that they typically lived to 33 years, and given that royalty had every advantage available at the time, it's reasonable to assume that common people lived even shorter lives.[12]

People are living longer in every region of the world. As shown in Figure 5.2, the world average in 1820 was 26 years. The United States averaged 39 years, and Africa and Asia averaged 23 years. Starting in 1900, life expectancy starting increasing everywhere, and now it's around 66 years. As recently as 1950, India and China, the world's two most populated countries, had average life expectancies of around 40 years. Now both are up to the mid-60s—an astonishing 50% increase in just half a century.[13]

If you wanted to pick the single greatest achievement in human history, doubling worldwide life expectancy in the past one hundred years might just be it. Even with this general sustained increase in life expectancy, some countries have had temporary drops due to warfare, sickness, or dramatic social change. The World Health

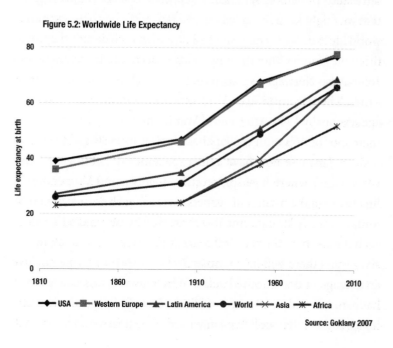

Figure 5.2: Worldwide Life Expectancy

Source: Goklany 2007

Organization identified sixteen countries that lost two or more years of life expectancy since 1990—most of them African countries ravaged by AIDS. The biggest losers have been Zimbabwe, Swaziland, and Botswana, each of which has lost ten years or more of life expectancy over the past two decades. South Africa, Zambia, and Kenya lost five or more years. Both the Ukraine and Iraq have lost several years due to dramatic social and political change—the fall of communism and the end of Saddam Hussein's rule.[14] Over a longer period of time, however, few countries lost ground. In the half century from 1955 until 2005, only three countries had a net loss of life expectancy: Swaziland, Zimbabwe, and Russia.[15] In the remaining 180+ countries, people live longer.

Studies of life expectancy have posed an interesting question: Is there an upper limit to life expectancy, or will humans continue to live longer? Well, not having time machines, we don't know for sure, but a study by demographers Jim Oeppen and James Vaupel suggests that we might keep living longer and longer.[16] They have examined world life expectancy rates since 1840, and in each decade they identified the country with the longest life expectancy. In the 1840s and 1850s it was Norwegians who, fueled by lutefisk, were living into their fifties. Then, from 1870 to 1940, it was New Zealanders, living to age seventy by 1940. After World War II, the Norwegians reclaimed their spot on top until the Japanese took it in 1980 and have held it since. Japanese now have a life expectancy of about eighty-five years. Here's where it gets interesting. Oeppen and Vaupel drew a line through the highest life expectancies in each decade, and they found a mostly straight line that increased by two and a half years each decade over the past 160 years. If this trend continues, in just sixty years there will be countries in the world whose people live an average of one hundred years. Who knows if this will actually happen, but with continued medical and technological advances, it's a good bet that we'll live longer for some time yet.

Christians Making a Difference

The Christian charity Mercy Ships has a really big boat that does a really big amount of good. Their boat, the *Africa Mercy*, is a floating five-hundred-foot-long hospital with six operating rooms and seventy-eight hospital beds. Mercy Ships provides state-of-the-art medical care for the poorest of the poor in the world. Founded in 1978, this ministry has performed over 32,000 surgeries, such as fixing cleft palates, removing cataracts, and orthopedic and facial reconstruction. They have performed more than 190,000 dental treatments and treated over 210,000 people in village medical clinics. They've taught 100,000 people in primary medical care, and delivered $60 million worth of medical equipment and supplies. They have even completed almost a thousand community development projects such as schools, clinics, orphanages, and water wells. All told, it's estimated that 1.9 million people worldwide have directly benefited from Mercy Ships.[17]

Infant Mortality

A key component of life expectancy in any society is its infant mortality rate—how many children die before their first birthday. It is usually measured as deaths per 1,000 live births. For example, an infant mortality rate of 100 would mean that 1 in 10 children die in their first year. Infant mortality is a good measure of how a society is doing overall because it reflects general levels of health and well-being.[18] In the United States, infant mortality rates have plummeted over the past one hundred years. As shown in Figure 5.3, in 1900, 16% of all children born did not live to their first birthday. That's 1 in 6 children! By 1940 this dropped to 4.7%, and now it's .7% or about 1 in 150 children. Given the extraordinary pain and heartache suffered by parents who lose their children, this change is perhaps more appreciated than any other single improvement discussed in this book.

In the United States, African-Americans have a very high infant mortality rate with 13.6 deaths per 1,000 live births. This is followed by Native Americans with 8.1, whites with 5.8, Hispanics with 5.6, and Asians at 4.9. Over the last century, infant mortality rates have

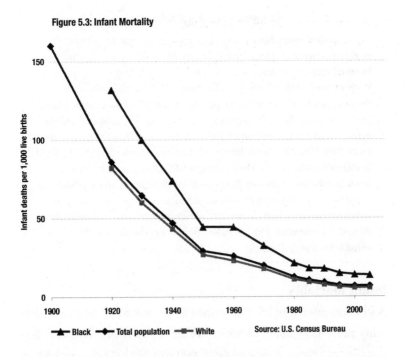

Figure 5.3: Infant Mortality

Infant deaths per 1,000 live births

▲ Black ◆ Total population ■ White   Source: U.S. Census Bureau

dropped for all racial and ethnic groups. For example, African-American infant mortality dropped from 131 in 1920 to 44 in 1960, to its current level of just under 14 per 1,000 live births.

Infant mortality rates have also fallen worldwide. Looking back in history, the infant mortality rate of ancient Rome is estimated to have been around 300, and among hunters and gathers it was 400 to 500. Europe in the Middle Ages had rates ranging from 150 to 300.[19] It is estimated that before industrialization, the infant mortality rate worldwide was about 200; now, however, it's closer to 50. Developed countries such as Sweden and France have the lowest rates, 2.8 and 4.4 respectively, and Sub-Saharan Africa has the highest rates at about 100. China and India, in particular, have made remarkable progress. In 1950, they both had infant mortality rates close to 200, and now China's rate is 33 and India's is 63.[20] During the fifty-year span from 1955 to 2005, infant mortality rates fell in every country worldwide; however, since 1990 they have actually risen in twenty-six countries (out of 186 countries measured), mostly due to the AIDS epidemic in Sub-Saharan Africa.[21]

Why have infant mortality rates fallen so dramatically worldwide? In most nations, both mothers and children have more and better food, safer water, better health care, and improved sanitation.[22] Effective health interventions include immunizations, oral rehydration for diarrhea, mosquito nets, and treatment of influenza.[23] Nonetheless, even with this remarkable progress, we should keep in mind that millions of infants die each year due to easily preventable causes.[24] Things are improving, but so much more can be done.

Christians Making a Difference

In 1982, Jeremiah Lowney, an orthodontist from Connecticut, felt challenged by his Catholic beliefs to do something for the extreme poor in the world, so he traveled to Port-au-Prince, Haiti, to provide free dental care. Given the lack of facilities and follow-up care, this meant mostly pulling out rotted teeth. Jeremiah continued these visits, working with Mother Teresa's Sisters of Charity. In 1985, Mother Teresa requested that he move his efforts to the rural, southwestern area of Haiti, an area even worse off in terms of health care. Jeremiah founded the Haitian Health Foundation (HHF), and for twenty-five years now it has provided public health, medicine, food, and educational support for the nearly quarter-million people living in this part of Haiti. HHF has focused particularly on the well-being of pregnant women and infants and, due to their efforts, the infant mortality rate in this region has fallen dramatically. When HHF first arrived, very few women breastfed their children; now 80% of them do (compared to only 3% in the rest of Haiti). Breastfeeding provides excellent nutrition for newborns. HHF has trained scores of local field agents to work with the rural villages and provide rudimentary health care. These efforts have dropped the rate of pneumonia deaths among children by 50% as well as decreased deaths due to dehydration. The main HHF clinic provides three or more medical checkups for 80% of the pregnant women in the region. While it's difficult to know exactly how many, the work of Jeremiah, his daughter Marilyn, and countless volunteers has saved the lives of numerous infants.[25]

Infectious Diseases

Infectious diseases aren't what they used to be. Throughout much of human history, infections and parasites were primary causes of death worldwide; however, most developed countries have virtually eliminated them.[26] To give a sense of how much things have changed, Figure 5.4 plots the incidents in the United States of tuberculosis, malaria, typhoid fever, whooping cough, measles, polio, and smallpox.[27] As you can see, the occurrences of these have dropped precipitously; in fact, two of them, polio and smallpox, are now virtually nonexistent. Previously, though, infectious diseases were a scourge. In 1900, almost half of all deaths in the United States resulted from tuberculosis, pneumonia, and diarrhea—maladies now easily treatable or preventable. As you read this section, you might be wondering why we should even be talking about the impact of these infectious diseases in the United States, since they affect relatively

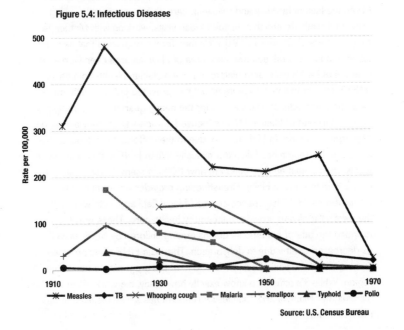

Figure 5.4: Infectious Diseases

Source: U.S. Census Bureau

few Americans. Well, that's the point. We've made so much progress in this area that we no longer even think about it, and instead we focus on things more troubling for society. As a result of forgetting what has gotten better and fixating on what is wrong, we maintain negative views about the state of the world even after substantial improvements are made.

Cancer

In contrast to many infectious diseases, cancer remains a real concern for many Americans. The incidence rate of cancer rose from 1975, when 400 people per 100,000 had cancer, to a peak in 1992, when 510 had it. At that point, the cancer rate started to decline to its current level of 456 cases per 100,000.[28] Figure 5.5 plots the incidence rates for seven different cancers since 1975. Rates of prostate, breast, lung, and colon cancer and non-Hodgkin's lymphoma increased

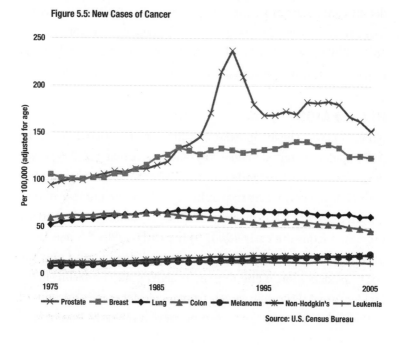

Figure 5.5: New Cases of Cancer

Source: U.S. Census Bureau

through about 1990 but have fallen or remained steady since. Rates of melanoma, a type of skin cancer, have continued to rise.

The biggest change with cancer, however, is not in how many people get it, but in how long people live once they do. People with cancer are living much longer now due to earlier detection and improved treatment.[29] In 1976, only 50% of people diagnosed with cancer lived longer than five years; now that number is 68%.[30] Before the 1970s, cancer survival rates were measured only for men (apparently women didn't become important until the mid-'70s), but in 1962, a scant 39% of white men diagnosed with cancer lived five years.

Some cancers are more lethal than others, but survival rates have gone up with pretty much all cancers. For example, in 1976, 70% of men diagnosed with prostate cancer lived for at least five years, and now it's a remarkable 99%. Likewise, the five-year survival rates for breast cancer and melanoma are now above 90%. Even the most deadly cancers are more survivable. The five-year survival rates for leukemia rose from 36% to 55%, and for lung cancer from 12% to 16%. While I pray that I and my family never get cancer, I would much rather have it now than even a couple of decades ago.

HIV and AIDS

No discussion of health in America can ignore HIV/AIDS. Since the AIDS epidemic started in the early 1980s, more than 570,000 people have died from it. Currently more than one million Americans live with HIV infection.[31] As shown in Figure 5.6, the number of new reported cases of AIDS diagnoses in the United States substantially increased from the early 1980s to the early 1990s.[32] Since 1993, however, new cases of AIDS have dropped steadily, and now the AIDS incidence rate is one-third of its high point. The decline in the incidence of AIDS results largely from medical therapies introduced in the mid-1990s that slow down or prevent the transition of HIV

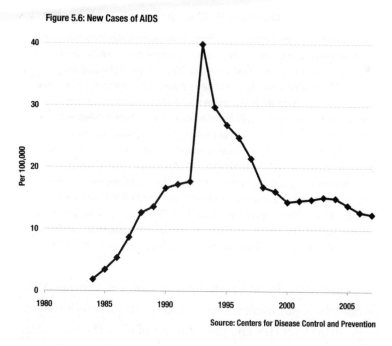

Figure 5.6: New Cases of AIDS

Per 100,000

Source: Centers for Disease Control and Prevention

into AIDS. The rate of new HIV cases has remained fairly steady since the mid-1990s.[33]

While AIDS advocates highlight the potential risk of HIV/AIDS for everyone, it's most concentrated in several subgroups of society. Men who have sex with other men represent a small portion of society, but they account for over half of new HIV diagnoses. A man who has sex with other men is forty times more likely than others to be diagnosed with the disease. African-Americans also have high rates of HIV. While they constitute 12% of the population, they account for almost half of the new HIV diagnoses. An African-American male stands a 1 in 16 chance of being diagnosed with HIV sometime in his life, and African-American females 1 in 30.[34]

Worldwide, the AIDS epidemic has followed a similar pattern as in the United States.[35] The number of adults newly diagnosed with HIV dropped from 3 million in 2001 to 2.7 million in 2007. The

---

Christians Making a Difference

The Catholic Medical Missionary Board believes and supports that every human life is valued, and its mission is to provide quality health care to people in need throughout the world. In 2009 alone, it shipped more than $250 million worth of medicine and medical supplies to its partners in developing countries, and provided 475 short-term and 73 long-term health-care volunteers. It also trains health-care workers in other countries and distributes information about best practices in public health.

CMMB focuses specifically on maternal and child health, country-specific diseases, and the worldwide HIV/AIDS epidemic. CMMB sets up programs to prevent pediatric and adult HIV infections via educational programs, and it provides care and treatment to HIV/AIDS patients to reduce their suffering and extend their lives. Since 2000, it has provided over $700,000 worth of anti-retroviral therapy medications to health-care partners working directly with women and children infected with AIDS.[37]

---

number of AIDS deaths has declined as well. Sub-Saharan Africa has been the region hardest hit; it now accounts for two-thirds of all people living with HIV and three-fourths of all AIDS deaths. Heterosexual intercourse is the primary means of HIV transmission in Sub-Saharan Africa, resulting in a large population of children born with HIV. Elsewhere in the world, however, HIV disproportionately affects men who have sex with other men, intravenous drug users, and sex workers.[36]

Substance Abuse

Americans' improving health even encompasses substance abuse. Let's start by talking about cigarettes. For whatever reason, I have very strong, negative feelings against smoking. While I sometimes have doubts about myself as a parent, I know that I have done at least one thing right in steering my sons away from smoking. Since an early age they heard that smoking is "gross" and "smelly." In fact, at one point I had to ease up with my anti-smoking rhetoric when my then five-year-old would march up to smokers in public and chew them out about hurting themselves and others. But it's not just me: Public health officials also view cigarette smoking as harmful. An estimated 25% of all men's deaths and 14% of women's deaths are linked to tobacco.[38]

Smoking got a big boost during World War II as free cigarettes were given to the troops,[39] and the number of cigarettes smoked by Americans (per capita) steadily rose into the 1960s.[40] Then, in 1964, the Surgeon General published a report warning about the dangers of smoking cigarettes, and ever since then smoking has declined. Now Americans smoke only 60% as many cigarettes per capita as in 1964. In the 1960s, more than 40% of adults regularly smoked, and now that number is down to less than 25%.[41] Worldwide, about one-quarter of all adults use tobacco. Europe has the most smokers, with one-third of all adults smoking.[42] Just under a quarter of adults in the Americas and Southeast Asia smoke, and 1 in 10 adults in Africa do.

With alcohol, Americans' consumption has remained roughly stable over the past one hundred years at between two and three gallons of pure alcohol a year. (Not that most of us drink it as pure alcohol. Rather, it's a common way to measure the amount of alcohol consumption. For example, a 12-ounce bottle of 5% beer would have .6 ounces of "pure" alcohol.) The lowest intake of alcohol was in the 1930s, after Prohibition, when American adults consumed less than two gallons. From there it steadily rose to 1980, when American adults drank 2.8 gallons in celebration of the demise of the disco era. Then it started falling. Currently American adults consume about 2.3 gallons a year, with about one-half coming from beer, one-third hard liquor, and one-sixth wine.[43]

Compared to other developed countries, Americans are relatively moderate drinkers. Luxemburg, France, Ireland, and the ironically named Hungary drink 50% more alcohol per capita than Americans. New Zealand, Canada, and Italy drink about the same amount we do. Mexico drinks substantially less.[44] According to the World Health Organization, Europe leads all regions by consuming an average of 2.3 gallons of pure alcohol a year. It is followed by the Americas with 1.8 gallons, the West Pacific with 1.4 gallons, and Africa with 1.1 gallons. The driest regions are Southeast Asia and the Eastern Mediterranean—they average less than a quart of alcohol a year.[45]

A good way to track the various substances abused by Americans comes from data measuring the behavior of high school seniors. As shown in Figure 5.7, the percentage of high school kids who smoke has dropped steadily over the past quarter century. In 1980, when I graduated from high school, 21% of high school seniors smoked— most of them doing so in front of their school and looking very cool. Now it's down to 11%. Likewise, binge drinking (having five drinks in a single setting) has declined. In 1980, 41% of seniors reported

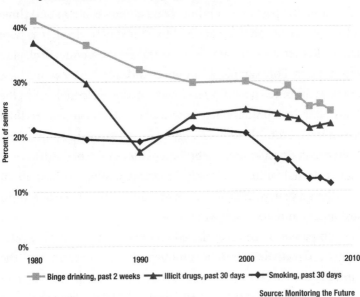

Figure 5.7: Substance Abuse Among High School Seniors

Binge drinking, past 2 weeks — Illicit drugs, past 30 days — Smoking, past 30 days

Source: Monitoring the Future

binge drinking in the previous two weeks, and now it's down to 25%. In contrast, rates of illicit drug use has bounced around somewhat. It dropped substantially from 1980 to 1990, rose somewhat through 2000, and has remained mostly stable since. Currently about 19% of high school seniors have smoked marijuana in the past thirty days, 1.9% have used cocaine, 1.4% have used inhalants, and 1.8% have used Ecstasy.[46]

Obesity—Some Bad News

So far in this chapter it's been almost all good news about health, but here's one problem that is getting worse, or, should I say, bigger: obesity. After smoking, obesity is the second leading preventable cause of death in America, killing an estimated quarter-million Americans each year.[47] Complications from obesity include heart attacks, strokes, diabetes, hypertension, osteoarthritis, sleep apnea, and some forms of cancers.[48] The estimated direct and indirect costs of obesity in America tops $100 billion a year.[49]

Using the body mass index chart, we can classify Americans into four groups: not overweight, overweight, obese, and extremely obese. Now, if you're squeamish, you might want to look away at this point. In 1960, as per Figure 5.8, 54% of Americans were not overweight, 32% were overweight, and 14% were obese or extremely obese. By 2006—billions of fast-food meals, pints of ice cream, and whatever else later—only 26% of Americans are not overweight. Thirty-four percent are overweight, and, drumroll please (or should I say drumstick), 40% of Americans are obese or extremely obese.

I write this not to judge others, for my own weight fluctuates across the entire "overweight" range. (Until not long ago, I thought that a pint of Ben and Jerry's ice cream was a single-serving size. Really.) Nonetheless, weight is a major public health problem in the United States. As with any problem, perhaps the first step is for Americans to realize they have a problem with weight. Somehow

Figure 5.8: Obesity Rates

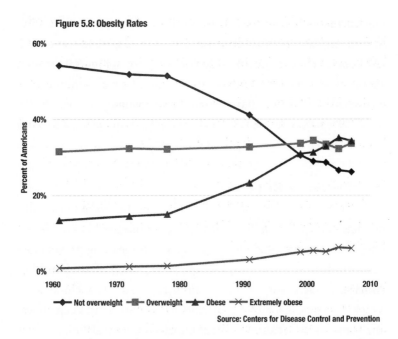

Source: Centers for Disease Control and Prevention

most of us think our weight is just fine. In a 2005 poll, 60% of Americans described themselves as being at the right weight, 6% said underweight, and only 34% said overweight.[50] Apparently we Americans like our food with a side order of denial.

Why don't you do this: Go online to find a body mass index calculator (simply Google "calculate BMI"), and look up your body mass index. If it's over 25 points, you're overweight; if it's over 30 points, you're officially obese; and if it's over 40 points, you've hit extreme obesity. At this point you might go through the stages of grief, including anger, denial, bargaining, depression, and finally acceptance. You might even decide that you're suddenly a public health expert, and the body mass index is constructed all wrong. Instead, if you're overweight or obese, accept that you have a problem and figure out what to do about it.[51] Doing something about it will, in the long run, only make you feel better.

Even our children are not immune from weight problems. Why in the world would we adults think that we don't pass along our bad habits to our children? In the late 1970s, only 6% of children between ages 6 to 17 were measured as overweight. Now it's 17%—nearly triple.[52] Even 11% of preschoolers are overweight.[53]

Worldwide, other countries don't even hold a pork chop to the United States. In other developed countries, an estimated 14% of people are obese—far less than the 40% of obese Americans.[54] Obesity affects one-quarter of Mexicans and British; one-fifth of New Zealanders and Australians; one-eighth of Spaniards, Germans, and Irish; and a measly 3% of Japanese and South Koreans (I don't think they're even trying).[55]

Hunger

As much as we Americans eat, it's hard to believe that there is hunger anywhere in the world, but there is. World hunger rates are often measured in terms of calories consumed. How many calories a given person needs varies by their age, gender, body size, and physical activity. People who are moderately active require anywhere from about 1,800 calories (for a small woman), to 3,100 calories (for a large man).[56] People can't even sustain light activity on much less than 1,200 to 1,800 calories a day.

In the last fifty years, the world's population has more than doubled, going from 3 billion people in 1960 to nearly 7 billion now.[57] You might assume this would mean hunger is more prevalent because there are so many more mouths to feed; however, worldwide hunger has steadily dropped. The worldwide average of calories consumed actually rose from 2,250 calories per person in 1960 to 2,800 calories today—a 25% increase. As shown in Figure 5.9, the number of calories consumed per capita in developing countries has steadily increased over the past fifty years—an average of 38% worldwide. Remarkably, China went from a below-starvation level

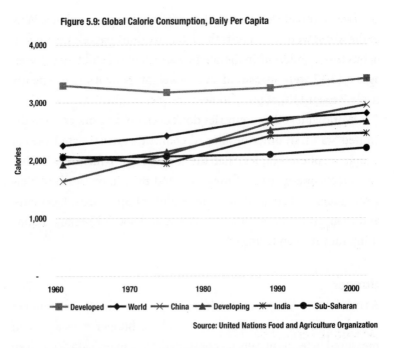

Figure 5.9: Global Calorie Consumption, Daily Per Capita

Source: United Nations Food and Agriculture Organization

of 1,640 calories in 1960 to a robust 2,950 calories today—an 80% increase. India increased 19%. Even Sub-Saharan Africa has witnessed some increase, albeit a very modest 7%.

Given this increase in calories consumed, it's no surprise that hunger rates have dropped. Currently, an estimated one billion people worldwide are undernourished, according to United Nations estimates.[58] Few people in developed countries, such as the United States, fit this description; however, an estimated 19% of people in developing countries are undernourished. It was even worse in the past. In 1945, an estimated 45% of the developing world was undernourished, and in 1980 it was 29%.[59] While today represents a substantial improvement over the past, there are, of course, still far too many hungry people.

Fewer people are hungry because food is much cheaper now. Since 1950, the price of basic food commodities has dropped an average of 75% because agriculture has become much more productive.[60] A single acre of cropland today produces about twice as much food as it did in the year 1900.[61] This productivity results from better irrigation, use of fertilizers and pesticides, and superior farm management skills.[62] We can appreciate today's agricultural productivity all the more by going back further in history. In the year 1490, a single acre of corn in North America yielded about ten bushels. By 1900, this was up to twenty-five bushels, and now it's around 120 bushels.[63] Also, nations are wealthier, meaning they can provide better infrastructure such as roads, storage bins, and processing plants.[64] As a result, it is easier and less expensive to move food from place to place. Wealth also means that nations can buy food that they can't grow for themselves. No longer do countries have to depend solely on what they or their neighbors can grow.[65]

Accidents and Disasters

Even accidental deaths are becoming less common. As you might guess, car crashes are the leading cause of accidental death in the United States. In 2006, 44,700 Americans died in motor vehicle accidents.[67] That is just a shade under the total number of U.S. battle deaths in the Vietnam War. Every twenty-five days about three thousand Americans die in motor vehicle accidents—about the number

---

Christians Making a Difference

Gleanings for the Hungry is a Christian ministry program within Youth With a Mission (YWAM). Located in the Central Valley of California, they accept excess fruit from local growers and packing houses. They then dry the fruit for twelve weeks during the summer, using the volunteer labor of eighty to one hundred young people at a time. In 2008 alone they dried over 7 million pounds of fruit! During the winter, they make dried soup mix from dehydrated vegetables. The dried fruit and soup mixes are shipped worldwide to feed people in food programs, schools, and orphanages.[66]

---

killed in the attack on the World Trade Center. Not only are people killed, but for every motor vehicle fatality, there are around one hundred injuries, some of them debilitating.[68] The good news? Driving is safer than ever. Figure 5.10 plots rates of accidental deaths, including motor vehicle accidents, since 1970, and today a person is only 60% as likely to die in a vehicle accident as thirty-five years ago.[69] This statistic actually underestimates the increase in driving safety because Americans are driving more miles now. In terms of miles driven, in 1925, there were 18 deaths for every 1 billion miles driven. By 1940, this had dropped to 10 deaths, and by 1960 it was about 5. Now it's under 2 deaths.[70] Do you want to drive to the store? Do it now, rather than in the past.

Driving is much safer now because cars have better safety features, roads are built better, driver's education is more effective, and better medical care is provided to those who have suffered vehicle accidents.[71] Also, driving laws are stricter. I realized this earlier this

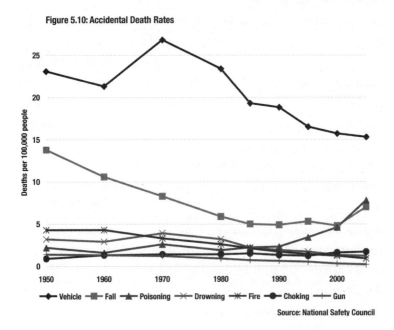

Figure 5.10: Accidental Death Rates

Source: National Safety Council

week when I took my sixteen-year-old son to get his driver's license. He passed the driving test just fine, but it will be twelve months before he's allowed by law to drive with someone in the car other than a family member. He is also limited in driving at night. I compare this to when I got my driver's license in 1979. I passed the test in the afternoon, and by evening I was driving the family van around full of screaming friends, touring local fast-food drive-thrus.

In addition to driving, flying has also become safer. Some people fear flying, which is understandable, given how much publicity accompanies plane accidents. They are typically front-page news. However, in 2006, only fifty people died in U.S. commercial plane accidents, and fewer than twenty-five did in each of the previous four years.[72] It's four times safer to fly a mile than it is to drive it (though one-mile flights are difficult to find). In fact, if you fly two thousand miles a year, you're as likely to die from an airplane falling on you while driving a car as you are flying on that commercial airline.[73] It's not just American airline carriers that are safer now; flying is safer worldwide. In the late 1980s, the global airline fatality rate ranged from .04 to .06 (per million passenger kilometers). In the past four years, it's down to .01 to .02.[74] On average, a passenger would have to take a commercial airline flight every day for 20,000 years before they died in a crash. By then, death might be a welcome escape from peanuts and pretzels.[75]

It's not just transportation that's safer. As shown in Figure 5.10, other forms of accidental deaths have declined as well. Americans are 15% to 50% as likely now, compared to the 1950s, to die from falls, drowning, fires, and guns. Society has worked hard at improving day-to-day safety. With fires it's not that we humans are suddenly less flammable. Rather, we have stronger safety measures such as smoke alarms and built-in sprinklers, as well as more effective fire departments.[76] Even work is getting safer due to more stringent regulations and employer training programs.[77] From 1970 to 1995, on-the-job fatalities dropped from 18 per 100,000 workers down to 4.[78] There are two types of accidents, however, that are getting worse: Choking deaths have gone up 80% since 1950, and poisonings are up 250%.[79] Yet again, we Americans have trouble with what we put into our mouths.

Even the weather is getting safer. In 1920, there were 242 weather-related deaths per million people worldwide, and now it's down to three—a remarkable 99% reduction. It's not that storms no longer blow; rather, we are better at adapting to weather. Also, more accurate weather forecasting enables us to prepare better, and wealthier nations have more to spend preparing for and reacting to weather emergencies. To illustrate the importance of wealth in surviving natural disasters, consider two recent hurricanes. In 2007 a category-5 hurricane hit the relatively well-prepared Yucatan in Mexico, and no one died. The next year, a category-5 hurricane hit the much poorer Burma, and 200,000 people died.[80] Death rates due to droughts and floods have also dropped more than 90% over the past one hundred years.[81]

How and When People Die

So far this chapter has dealt with specific health problems, but let's step back a bit and examine general trends in how Americans die. The eight leading causes of death for Americans are heart disease, cancer, stroke, lung disease, accidents, diabetes, flu and pneumonia, and suicide. To illustrate how each of these has changed, I took the annual death rate associated with each malady in the year 1960, and I gave it a value of 100. From there I tracked changes with each death rate relative to its 1960 score. For example, if a score drops from 100 to 50, that means a death rate dropped to half of its 1960 level.

As shown in Figure 5.11, three of these leading causes of death are about as common now as they were fifty years ago.[82] Cancer death rates increased somewhat in the 1980s and 1990s, but they have

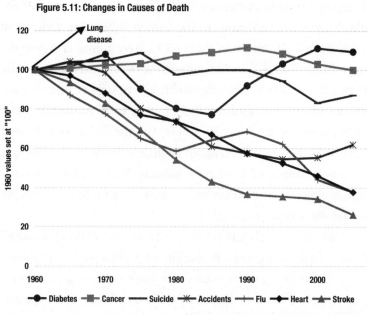

Figure 5.11: Changes in Causes of Death

Source: Centers for Disease Control and Prevention

since dropped back to their 1960 levels. Diabetes deaths dropped steadily through 1985, and then started climbing, and are now 10% more prevalent than in 1960. Suicide rates have slowly dropped since the early 1970s. Four causes of death have declined significantly—accidents (61% of their 1960 rate), heart disease (38%), flu and pneumonia (also 38%), and strokes (26%). Only one of these types of death increased substantially—lower respiratory disease. From 1960 to 2005, the death rate attributed to lower respiratory disease skyrocketed by 345%. It increased so much that to include it in Figure 5.11 would require a line that would end about a foot above the book that you're reading right now, so I just pointed its direction with a short arrow.

While we're on the topic of death, let's get really practical and figure out how you're going to die. I don't mean the exact circumstances of your death, like some guy named Colonel Mustard bumping you off in the library. Rather, how do Americans die? For illustrative purposes, suppose the United States were a village of 1,000 people. As shown in Figure 5.12, over a quarter would die from heart disease (254) and almost another quarter would die from cancer (232). After these two big killers, strokes, lung disease, and accidents would kill about 50 people each. Alzheimer's and diabetes would kill about 30 people, and the flu/pneumonia and kidney diseases would kill about 20 people. Fewer than 15 people would die from suicide, blood poisoning, liver disease, hypertension, homicide, and Parkinson's disease. In addition, 186 people would die of other causes.[83]

Of course, not all Americans are at equal risk of these maladies. Some people have genetic propensities toward a particular disease (e.g., Alzheimer's), while others may work in hazardous settings. Men are more likely to die from Parkinson's disease, liver disease,

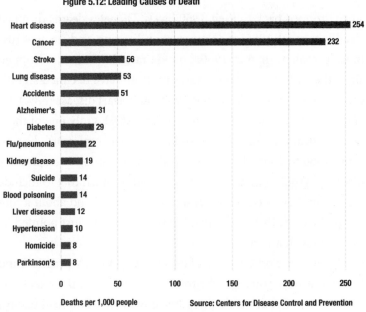

Figure 5.12: Leading Causes of Death

Deaths per 1,000 people — Source: Centers for Disease Control and Prevention and—wait for it—unintentional accidents. African-Americans die more often from diabetes, hypertension, and kidney disease, and Native Americans suffer more liver disease. On the other hand, Asian-Americans are less likely to die from accidents, Alzheimer's disease, liver disease, and lung disease. As such, you could get a more precise estimate of how you'll die if you factor in some personal information. But the information in Figure 5.12 gives you a general understanding of what to look forward to.

Now that we've established how you'll die, let's figure out when. Here's a hint: The longer you have lived already, the older the age that you can expect to live to. Figure 5.13 plots American life expectancy as a function of current age. Baby boys start out with seventy-five years, and baby girls eighty years.[84] Life expectancy goes up a few days or weeks for every year lived through age sixty-five, and after that it goes up much more quickly. Me? I'm forty-eight years old,

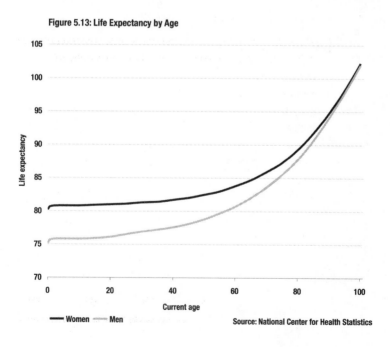

Figure 5.13: Life Expectancy by Age

Source: National Center for Health Statistics

so I'm looking at an average of seventy-eight years. If, however, I do make it to seventy-eight years, I can expect another ten years of life. Online there are various life-expectancy estimators that will give you more precise estimates based on your personal information. Some of them even calculate how many days you have left to live. Now that's motivation. Are you having trouble getting up in the morning? Look up how many mornings you have left.

This chapter, perhaps more than any other in the book, is chock-full of good news. Americans and people around the world are living longer, healthier lives. Oh sure, there's the occasional bit of gravy-covered bad news, but most of the changes in global health are encouraging if not astonishing. Things have gotten so much better that perhaps the only thing we can really gripe about with our health is that we weren't born in the future, because things might be even better then.

CHAPTER 6

ARE WE STRESSED AND UNHAPPY?

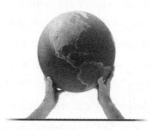

Most Americans say they are generally happy.
—*Gallup poll*[1]

The more one has, the more one wants.
—*Emile Durkheim*[2]

We seriously overestimate how much time we spend on work, and we dramatically underestimate how much free time we have at our disposal.
—*Robert Putnam, sociologist*[3]

Happiness

This book has so far focused on mostly objective measures of how people are doing, exploring such questions as, Do you have a job? How far did you go in school? Are you dead? However, most people—myself certainly included—spend a lot of time thinking about more subjective questions that revolve around the basic question of "Am I happy?" There is a lot of data about happiness levels in our country and the world. In this chapter, I explore these general issues of happiness and well-being. After reading this, you may still not know if you're happy, but you'll have a better sense of what is going on with everyone else.

When researchers want to know if people are happy, they usually just ask them. Now, I realize there are larger, philosophical issues about whether humans can ever truly know their own inner condition, but for now let's just take people's self-reported happiness at face value and look at how it has changed over time.

In general, most Americans are happy. Since the mid-1940s, survey researchers have asked us the following question: "Generally speaking, how happy would you say you are—very happy, fairly happy, or not happy?"[4] As you can see in Figure 6.1, the great majority of Americans report being "very happy" or "fairly happy." In fact, the highest levels of happiness have occurred in the recent years, when up to 55% of Americans described themselves as "very happy." Over the

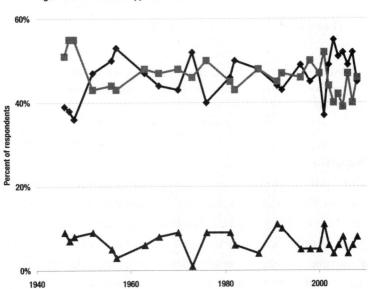

Figure 6.1: Americans' Happiness

past sixty years, only between 3% and 11% of Americans have been "not happy." One of the low points of happiness came in the year 2001, right after the 9/11 attacks, when "not happy" levels reached 11%.[5]

While overall fairly happy, Americans are not equally happy with every area of their lives. In a 2009 Gallup poll, respondents ranked their feelings about different areas from 1 = "not at all satisfied" to 10 = "extremely satisfied." As shown in Figure 6.2, Americans are most satisfied with their families, friends, and religion/spirituality. Each one of these areas scored an average of 8 or higher; in fact, fully 57% of respondents gave a family satisfaction score of 10 (maybe this scale should have gone up to 11). The two areas that rated lowest were careers and money, each ranking an average of 6 or below. This suggests that interpersonal relationships are a more reliable source of satisfaction than is work—a point that I'll pick up again in the closing chapter.

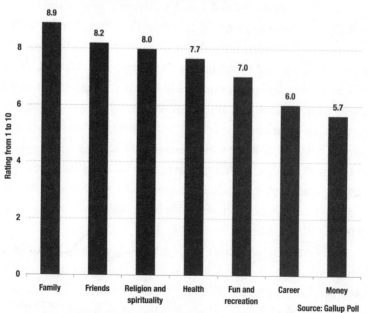

Figure 6.2: Satisfaction With Different Areas of Life

Source: Gallup Poll

Americans' happiness levels change with age. We start out very happy in our young adulthood, from around the ages of 18 to 24. From there, however, average happiness drops over the next few decades of life until people reach about fifty years old. At that point, happiness levels start rising, and they continue to through the eighties.[6] That's right: Life starts getting happier in the middle-aged years. This pattern of happiness over time has been linked to changes in social responsibilities. Young adults are weighed down with kids, careers, and mortgages, but by fifty, many people's careers are somewhat settled and their kids are maybe less work than they used to be. Also, people come to terms with what they have and haven't accomplished in life.[7] With age people feel less anger and stress, and they enjoy life more.[8] I just turned forty-eight this year, so if I fit into this normal cycle, I could look at my life in one of two ways: either "it doesn't get much worse than this" or "who's ready to have some fun!"

Studies have examined levels of happiness and well-being worldwide by asking people to rate their lives from 1 to 10, with 1 representing the worst possible life imaginable and 10 the best. In a recent Gallup study, the most satisfied countries averaged scores of 7 to 8—they included countries in North America and Western Europe, Japan, Australia, and Saudi Arabia.[9] The happiest place on earth? That would be Disneyland, but Denmark comes in second, scoring 8 on the 10-point scale. (Imagine if they built a Disneyland in Denmark; no one would ever leave!) The least-satisfied countries, ranging from 3 to 4.5, included countries in Sub-Saharan Africa, Haiti, and Cambodia. The most unhappy place? Togo, in West Africa. (Motto: "Who is Mickey Mouse?")

Why are some countries happier than others? Wealth matters. The happiest countries are also among the richest. Increased wealth, however, has its greatest effect in poorer countries. For example, there is a marked difference in happiness levels between countries averaging $2,000 in annual per-capita income versus $1,000. A $1,000 increase in income makes much less difference among wealthier countries, such as a country averaging $21,000 versus another one averaging $20,000. In fact, the difference in happiness between $2,000 and $1,000 is about the same magnitude as that between a $40,000 country and a $20,000 country.[10] In other words, the percentage increase matters more than the actual dollar increase.

Freedom of choice and expression also matter. The World Value Survey found that this was the second biggest happiness factor after income. Countries scored the highest levels of subjective well-being when their citizens had more control over their lives—both in what they did and said. For example, Latin American and Eastern European countries have similar, mid-range income levels, but Latin American countries have a much greater sense of well-being. Their citizens also report having more choice and control over their lives than people in the formerly Communist Eastern Europe.[11]

While some countries are much happier than others, it appears that most countries are getting happier over time. The World Value Survey has collected data about happiness since the early 1980s. It has long-term data for fifty-two countries (which are mostly developed countries), and it found that life satisfaction scores rose in forty-five of them, with an increase of about 7% on average. This suggests that, indeed, life is getting better in most places, at least according to people's perceptions.[12] Life satisfaction scores also went up more in poorer countries than wealthier countries. In recent decades, countries throughout the world have enjoyed increased wealth, democratization, and social tolerance, so it's no surprise that global happiness has risen during that time as well.[13]

Does Money Buy Happiness?

At this point you may be thinking that money indeed buys happiness. But let's examine the relationship between money and happiness a little more closely. It's no surprise that many Americans think they would be happier if they had more money. The Pew Foundation regularly asks Americans "Do you now earn enough money to lead the kind of life you want?" Currently, 45% of Americans say yes, but 55% say no, and this ratio has been mostly stable since the early 1990s, when the question was first asked.

How much money do Americans need to be happy? When asked, Americans report "needing" about 40% more than they currently have—regardless of how much they currently have. So a person making $20,000 a year thinks they'll be happy with $28,000, and a person who makes $100,000 wants $140,000. Since the amount needed to be happy increases faster than people's incomes, it means that even the very wealthy will never feel that they have enough money to be happy.[14]

Generally speaking, wealth is a relative concept. We get used to what we have, and we want more. After all, nicer things are always available. Yesterday's luxuries become today's necessities and tomorrow's relics.[15] One study illustrated this adaptation process by identifying twenty-four big-ticket items, such as owning a house and taking fancy vacations. It asked respondents how many of these twenty-four items one would need to live a good life, and the average answer was 4.3. Sixteen years later, the researchers re-interviewed the same people as before, and this time they answered 5.4 items.[16] As they got older, they thought that the good life entailed more and more things. I've seen this process in my own life as well. Going from a graduate student to an assistant professor more than doubled my income, but I can guarantee you that I wasn't twice as happy. Now we own a big house in a nice neighborhood, but sometimes we miss our old, cute little house in a not-so-great neighborhood.

People want money not just for the cool stuff it buys, but also because it makes them feel validated. In general, Americans believe in a just world, that people get what they deserve and deserve what they get. Based on this, it's easy (though not necessarily accurate) to assume that somebody with more money must be doing something right. This affirming nature of money can give us a sense of accomplishment and rightness.[17]

Because of this, we think money will make us happier, but is this true? Two acclaimed economists, Angus Deaton and Nobel Prize winner Daniel Kahneman, examined this question with a study of 450,000 Americans.[18] To begin with, they distinguished between two types of happiness: emotional well-being and life evaluation. Emotional well-being, based on feelings of joy, is measured by asking people how often they smile and laugh, and how often they do not feel stress, sadness, and anger. Life evaluation is more cognitive, and it's measured by having people evaluate their lives from 0, the worst possible life, to 10, the best possible life.

Kahneman and Deaton plotted how much both emotional well-being and life evaluation changed with household income. They found that the more money a person makes, the higher life-evaluation score they report. For example, Americans earning $20,000 a year rated their lives at 5.8 out of 10, but those making $200,000 rated their lives at 7.5. Having more money does lead us to think that our lives are better; however, there is a different pattern with our feelings. Kahneman and Deaton found that feelings of well-being increased with income through about $75,000 a year, but then the increase stopped and feelings of well-being leveled off. So people making $75,000 a year felt happier than those making $20,000, but people making $200,000 a year did not feel any happier than those making $75,000.

Put differently, having more money increases feelings of happiness at lower levels of income but not higher levels. This appears to happen because at lower levels, increased income takes care of life's essentials, such as having enough to eat, a safe place to stay, and suitable medical care.[19] Middle levels of income can help deal with life's misfortunes, such as chronic medical problems, divorce, and being alone.[20] Middle income also provides some leisure. However, after a certain point—estimated to be at about $75,000—more money just means having more stuff to take care of, and it stops making people happier.

This pattern of findings fits with the ideas of David Platt, a pastor of a large church in Birmingham, Alabama.[21] In his book, *Radical: Taking Back Your Faith from the American Dream,* Platt seeks to separate Christianity from the American Dream. He writes, "The American dream radically differs from the call of Jesus and the essence of the Gospel." According to Platt, while the American Dream emphasizes upward mobility, Christianity calls for downward mobility—giving ourselves away, not thinking of ourselves as better than others, and serving others. He calls for well-to-do American Christians to live on about $50,000 a year and give everything else away. While Platt makes his case in terms of spirituality, what he says also fits with social scientific research. If you want to feel good, maybe give yourself a raise from what Platt suggests, but after around $75,000 a year, you don't need any more, so you might as well give it away—which will make you feel even better.[22]

Christians Making a Difference

It's standard fare in rock music for bands to call for changing the world, but one of my favorite groups in college, Resurrection Band, has given their lives to it. Not only do they seriously rock, but many of its members have lived and participated with Jesus People USA, an intentional Christian community on the North Side of Chicago. About five hundred people live together, placing all their goods and properties into a single fund so they may more effectively help each other and people outside of their community. This pooling of money allows them to provide extensively for homeless women and children. Their ministries include providing housing for up to two hundred people in need, an overnight women's drop-in shelter, and an alternative youth center to keep kids off the streets.[23]

Suicide

Perhaps the polar opposite of happiness and satisfaction is suicide.[24] Suicide rates in the United States have generally fallen over the past fifty years. In 1950, there were 13.2 suicides each year per 100,000 people, but by 2005 this number had dropped to 10.9—an 18% decline.[25] Guns account for about half of all suicides, followed by suffocation and poisoning. As shown in Figure 6.3, men commit suicide far more than women. Through age sixty, men's suicide rates are about three to four times higher, and after age sixty the numbers diverge even more, with women's suicide rates dropping at the same time men's skyrocket. Men who live to ninety are more than ten times more likely than women to commit suicide. It is suggested that men commit suicide more often because women are more effective in dealing with feelings of depression and despair, such as by talking to a friend or clergy member, whereas men will let it build up until it's unbearable.[26]

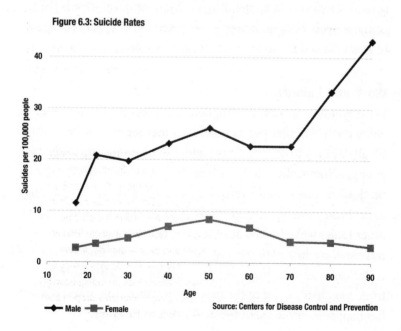

Figure 6.3: Suicide Rates

Source: Centers for Disease Control and Prevention

Suicide rates vary by region of the country, with the highest rates found in the sparsely populated Rocky Mountain states of Utah, Colorado, Wyoming, and Montana. Some of the lowest rates are in the population-dense corridor between Boston and Philadelphia, with suicide rates about two to three times less than that of some of the Rocky Mountain states.[27] This regional difference has been linked to greater availability of firearms in rural areas. Since guns are the preferred method of suicide, especially among men, the areas with more guns per household, such as the Rocky Mountain states, also have more suicides.[28]

The global suicide rate worldwide is about 50% higher than that in the United States, at 16 per 100,000 people. This translates to about one million suicides a year worldwide. Furthermore, international suicide rates appear to have risen in the past forty-five years, up by as much as 60%.[29] The countries with the highest suicide rates include those in Eastern Europe, while those with the lowest are in Latin America and several places in Asia. Generally speaking, suicide rates are higher in countries with indigenous peoples, such as the Aboriginal populations in Australia and the Inuit in Canada's arctic north.[30]

Work and Leisure

What good are health, wealth, and happiness if we're too busy to enjoy them? Popular perception holds that we Americans go full-tilt all day only to collapse at the end.[32] Even among my students—young, vibrant college kids—I frequently hear complaints of being tired, worn down, and overextended. Each generation continues to get busier and busier, right? Wouldn't you know it, like so many other topics we've looked at so far, our negative perceptions about busyness are just plain wrong. It turns out that, on average, we Americans are spending less time working and have more leisure time now than we did in the past. In fact, this drop in work hours has happened throughout the developed world.

Christians Making a Difference

In 2003, Jennifer was considering suicide. She was addicted to pain pills and was reeling from the death of her brother. Today, she is happily married with two children and finishing her college degree. What happened to Jennifer? Mercy Ministries. It is a long-term residential program aimed at helping troubled young women between the ages of thirteen and twenty-eight. This ministry provides six months of treatment at no charge, and the treatment includes counseling, nutrition education, life-skills training, fitness training, and educational opportunities. The goal of Mercy Ministries is for each young woman to not only complete the program, but also discover the purpose for her life and bring value to her community. This is accomplished in an environment that stresses excellence, accountability, and, most of all, unconditional love. Mercy Ministries has locations throughout the U.S. as well as in Canada, New Zealand, and the U.K. In thirty years, they have helped thousands of girls and women, more than 90% of whom have reported that Mercy Ministries transformed their lives and restored their hope.[31]

Economist Angus Maddison has estimated the annual work hours since 1870 for five major countries.[33] As shown in Figure 6.4, the average workweek has dropped in the United States, the United Kingdom, France, Germany, and Japan. For example, Americans worked nearly 3,000 hours a year in 1870, 1,800 hours in 1970, and just over 1,600 hours today.[34] The French dropped from almost 3,000 hours in 1870 to about 1,550 hours now, and even the famously hardworking Japanese dropped from almost 3,000 hours to about 2,000 hours. In 1900, most employed Americans worked ten hours a day, six or seven days a week; now it's eight hours a day, five days a week, and we have more holidays, vacations, sick days, and personal leave.[35]

We work fewer hours for various reasons. Workers these days have better education, more technology, and better tools and skills; this means we can produce more goods, services, and information in less time, reducing the need for working extended hours.[36] Also, since the 1950s, our changing social values, fueled by labor unions,

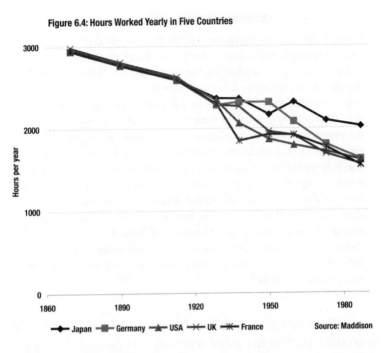

Figure 6.4: Hours Worked Yearly in Five Countries

Source: Maddison

Japan — Germany — USA — UK — France

have come to accept the forty-hour workweek as the norm.[37] Incidentally, despite its widespread acceptance now, not all approved of the forty-hour week initially. Critics argued that workers would abuse the reduced workload by spending more time in saloons. Also, they argued, the shortened workweek would block the more ambitious workers.[38]

The young and the old have experienced the greatest reduction in work hours. Young people today spend more time in education, meaning they enter the labor market at a later age. Also, labor laws have done away with most exploitation of child workers in America, which was a serious problem earlier in our history. In 1820, about half the workers in many Rhode Island factories and mills had not yet reached their eleventh birthday.[39] In 1900, an estimated 120,000 children worked in Pennsylvania mines and factories, many of them starting at age eleven. Reformer Marie Van Vorse took a job at one mill in 1903, and she found children as young as six or seven working twelve-hour shifts.[40]

Correspondingly, older workers are retiring earlier. A century ago, retirement at any age was a luxury. In 1900, only 15% of elderly workers had retired, by 1950 it was up to 50%, and now it's 70% or more.[41] Social security benefits have allowed most people over age 65 to retire. This has prompted a change in how Americans view work. A century ago, it was a lifelong activity, done until the worker could no longer do it. Now it's a phase of life (albeit an extended one) between schooling and retirement.[42]

Workers in the middle of their careers work about the same amount as before. Married men between the ages of 25 and 54 saw a slight decrease in hours worked between the 1960s and 2001.[43] And many women have entered the labor force and are staying in it longer. It's not so much that employed women work longer hours; rather, more women are working. As such, women now spend ten to thirteen hours a week longer in paid employment than in past decades. The rise in two-income families has resulted in some families spending more time working than they used to.[44]

Nonetheless, Americans' overall work hours have dropped, which has created an increase in leisure time. Leisure in this context measures time left over after paid work, child care, sleeping, eating, and education. Leisure activities include watching television, reading, playing sports, socializing, using the computer, exercising, and sitting by the pool being fed grapes by a loved one.[45] Researchers measure leisure time using time diaries, which are coding sheets used by respondents to record how they spend their time. Currently, the average American has thirty to forty hours of leisure time a week.[46] This is much more than in the past. In the 1880s, Americans averaged only about eleven hours of leisure a week.[47] From 1965 to 2003, leisure time increased for men by 7.9 hours and women 6 hours.[48]

Sociologist John Robinson concludes that "Americans now have more free time than at any point in the nation's history."[49]

Not only do we spend less time working outside the home, we also spend a lot less time doing household work such as cooking and cleaning.[50] In 1965, Americans averaged 17.5 hours a week of housework, and by 1995 it was down to 13.7 hours. Women, especially, have seen a decline, doing an average of twelve fewer hours of housework a week than in past decades.[51]

A long-term sociological study of a Midwestern city documents this change. In 1924, 87% of the married women spent four or more hours a day doing housework. By 1973 it was down to 43%, and by 2000 it was down to 14%.

We do less housework because the work is much more easily done. Think of your refrigerator (if you weren't already). Because of that big box in your kitchen, you need to shop only once a week instead of every day or two. Likewise, dishwashers, garbage disposals, washing machines and dryers, microwave ovens, and vacuum cleaners all save a lot of time. Imagine going a week without these appliances. Even heating the house has gotten easier. A century ago, residents in the colder states spent an estimated six hours a week in winter shoveling coal into their furnaces.[52] Now we just turn up the thermostat. Household appliances save so much time that when they first became popular in the 1960s, *Life* magazine published an article warning that Americans would have too much leisure time. It proclaimed that "Americans now face a glut of leisure," and the task ahead was "How to Take Life Easy."[53]

Not only is housework easier to do, but we have less to do because Americans have fewer children now than in the past, and nothing creates housework like children. In 1960, Americans had 23.7 children a year per 1,000 people. Now it's down to 13.9. (By my rough estimation as a parent, children double the amount of difficulty in our lives, but they triple the joy. We should keep this ratio in mind.)

This discussion of leisure raises an interesting question. If we have more free time on our hands, why do we feel so much busier? Technology serves as a double-edged sword here. It makes life more efficient, but it also allows us to fill more of our day with other stuff.[54] With computers we're constantly engaging the world, and with cell phones we're always available to others. Several months ago I got off a plane and saw a man standing in the boarding line. He had an open laptop computer in one hand and fast food in the other, and he was kicking his carry-on forward as the line moved. What was the critical matter that required him to be online? He was checking his Facebook account.

Technology also means that we're not slowed down by rote activities. This sounds good at first, but we may find that we miss them. A car means not having to walk, a dishwasher means not having to wash by hand, and a dryer means not having to hang up clothes. While time-consuming, these rote tasks can be mentally relaxing as they give our minds time to wander. Not doing them can thus impose mental costs.

Being too busy also conveys a certain status and cache.[55] Achieving the American Dream means hard work, and we convey our success to others by indicating that we are overwhelmed with stuff to do. If we have free time, then we're obviously not doing something that we could be doing. I've encountered this busy-as-a-status-symbol mentality in my own work. During the school year, I put in my eight to ten hours, five days a week, doing research, teaching, and professional service. During the summer, however, I'm not actually paid, and there is no teaching or service work, so I focus on research. After much trial and error, I have found that I get the most done when I write for four to five hours in the morning, five days a week. Any more than that is counterproductive because I lose focus, and the drop in my writing quality makes it not worth it. This routine has been wonderfully productive for me, but it has caused a problem. When I tell others about my work routine during the summer, or when they see me done for the day at about lunchtime, they sometimes react with bewilderment and scorn. How can I be a serious scholar if I'm not working the whole day? Am I taking things seriously? It doesn't matter that this summer routine maximizes my productivity, I still feel a little guilty about it.

Ultimately, busyness is essentially optional.[56] Yes, we need food on the table and a roof over our heads, but most of us go far, far beyond this. Consider this comparison between money and time.[57] Suppose that someone earns a million dollars a year, and they spend it lavishly—having only the best and most luxurious things. As a result, they have no money left over. Are they, in fact, poor? Most people would view excessive consumption of this hypothetical person and answer no. So it might be with time. We each start with 168 hours a week, and, after sleeping and working, we have about sixty to seventy hours a week left over to manage our lives. If we take on too many discretionary activities, do we really have too little time? For most us, our sense of being overwhelmed appears to be a self-inflicted wound.

Television Watching

Speaking of self-inflicted wounds, let's talk about television. It is Americans' number-one favorite leisure activity.[58] Just how much television do Americans watch? A bucket load. According to Nielsen figures, the average American spends over 37 hours a week watching television.[59] This number is so high that I actually read the report several times just to make sure I hadn't misunderstood it. Television viewing steadily increases with age. As shown in Figure 6.5, kids, teenagers, and young adults watch between 25 and 30 hours of television a week, and senior citizens average more than 50 hours. If we add this up, the average American watches about 2,000 hours of television a year. Over a lifetime, someone living to age 75 will

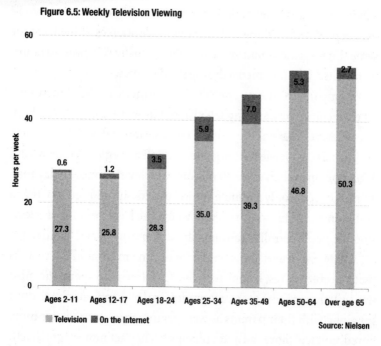

Figure 6.5: Weekly Television Viewing

Television   On the Internet

Source: Nielsen

have spent approximately 140,000 hours—about 15 years—watching television. Hmm, I'm pretty sure that's not on people's bucket lists. (See the Grand Canyon, check. Go skydiving, check. Spend fifteen years watching television, check.)

The Kaiser Family Foundation has tracked young people's media consumption since 1999. In their 2004 study, they found that kids (from 8 to 18) averaged nearly 6.5 hours of media time a day. This included television, music, computers, and video games. At that point, the researchers predicted that kids' media use had topped out because, after going to school, sleeping, and other basic activities, there just wasn't much more time left. Wrong. When they repeated the study in 2009, they found that young people's media consumption had increased to 7.5 hours a day. The top time-takers were television (4.5 hours), music and audio (2.5), computers (1.5), and video games (1.25). African-American and Hispanic youth consume about 50% more media (over

9 hours) than do white youth (just over 6 hours). Because young people are adept at multitasking—viewing multiple sources of media at the same time—some would argue that they actually consume 10 hours, 45 minutes' worth of media during the day. Wow.

Compared to the rest of the world, Americans hold their own when it comes to watching television, but we're not quite the best. For whatever reason, the world's most serious television watchers are clustered in Eastern Europe in the Balkan region. Serbians and Macedonians watch 15 to 30 minutes of television more a day than we do. Greece is only a minute behind us, closely followed by Croatia and Hungary. The countries that watch the least amount of television include Australia, Taiwan, China, Venezuela, and Thailand.[60]

Okay, we Americans spend a lot of time in front of a screen. Is that a problem? Yes, it appears to be. Children who spend the most time watching media get worse grades, are less happy at school, don't get along with their parents as well, get into more trouble, are more bored, and feel more sad and unhappy.[61] They act more aggressively, eat more junk food, and, among girls, have more eating disorders.[62] These correlations don't necessarily imply causation. It could also be that kids may retreat into television if they are already unhappy or are having trouble in school. Still, it's hard not to believe that excessive television watching is harmful for children.

It's not just how much we watch, it's also *what* we watch. The world portrayed on television is very different from real life. In evening television dramas, only one-third of the characters are women, 3% are old, 1% Hispanic, and 10% married.[63] Only 6% of television characters convey a religious identity (compared to over two-thirds of Americans), and television characters drink much more alcohol than real people.[64] Television is also very violent. Think about it. How many murders have you seen in real life? Hopefully none. How many murders have you seen on television? Probably thousands. An estimated six out of ten television programs display graphic violence, and in them the aggressor usually goes unpunished and the victim shows little sign of pain. A television character is eight times more likely to be victimized by a violent crime than a real person.[65] In children's shows, violence is usually portrayed as funny.[66]

Television is also full of sex. (Now that's a surprise!) In an average prime-time hour, there are fifteen sexual acts, words, or innuendos. A year of television shows young, unmarried television characters having sex about 20,000 times, and they almost never catch a disease or get pregnant.[67]

Understandably, parents worry that their children will imitate the people they see on television. However, what may be the bigger problem is that children—and adults—will think that television represents how most other people act. If we spend thousands of hours a year watching a violent, sex-driven, irreligious world, won't we start to assume that's how the real world works? We appear to, at least with violence. People who watch more television tend to overestimate how much violence happens in the world. Among children, those who watch the most television are more likely to think that someone will hurt them if they go outside.[68] Television leads us to view the world as a mean, frightening place.

What, then, should parents do? At the very least, we should create and enforce three types of rules for our children: *what* they can watch, *when* they can watch, and *how much* they can watch. Families that impose these three types of rules have children significantly more likely to be engaged in school.[69] Thankfully, more and more parents are doing this. In 1998, 55% of American families had these types of rules, and by 2006 it was 63%. (In fact, it might be a good idea for us adults to impose these rules on ourselves as well.)

CHAPTER 7

WHAT ABOUT CRIME AND WAR, FREEDOM AND FAITH?

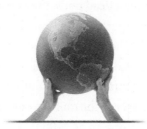

The United States incarcerates more people than any country in the world.

—*The Pew Center on the States*[1]

Americans have a decidedly negative outlook about crime [despite] violent crime as well as property crime having leveled off at extremely low numbers.

—*Gallup poll*[2]

Worldwide, "democracy has scored impressive gains in recent times."

—*Freedom House*[3]

Although Americans may be, for the most part, employed, well-educated, and healthy, we surely can't deny that violence and law-lessness are all around us, right? I mean, one glance at the news and it's clear that we're surrounded by war, murder, rape, and countless other acts of violence. And this doesn't even touch on theft, racism, and other illegal or immoral acts. Things are clearly getting worse when it comes to crime and war, aren't they? Well . . .

Crime

With crime, perhaps more than any other area of life, Americans' perceptions are out of line with reality. We're convinced that things are getting worse, but crime rates have actually plummeted over the last thirty years. Let's examine this change by starting with homicide, probably the most accurately measured type of crime. (After all, when someone finds a dead body, they usually tell the authorities about it. We even report it when someone is just missing.[4]) As indicated in Figure 7.1, homicide rates since 1900 peaked in two different periods: the mid-1930s and the 1980s.[5] At both of these times, the annual murder rate rose to about 10 murders per 100,000 people. Since 1990, however, the murder rate has steadily dropped, and it's now about 6 murders per 100,000—its lowest rate in 40 years. Similarly, other types of violent crime have steadily dropped since 1990, including forcible rape, aggravated assault, and robbery.[6]

How likely are you yourself to be murdered? Your risk depends on who you are. Men are almost four times more likely to be murdered than women, and blacks are more than six times more likely than whites.[7] Teenagers are three times more likely than people in their late forties and seven times more likely than people over age sixty-five.

There is some irony here. Older people worry the most about victimization, but they are at the lowest risk. So if you're a middle-aged white woman, go crazy; you're bulletproof.

Burglary rates have also dropped. As shown in Figure 7.1, they rose in the 1960s, peaked in the 1970s, and have fallen steadily since 1980. Burglary rates today are 45% what they were in 1980. Other property crimes, including general theft and car theft, have also declined.[8]

Figure 7.1: Homicide and Burglary Rates

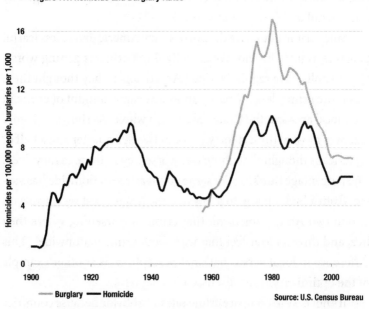

So why the big drop in crime rates over the last few decades? Scholars have given various explanations. Some attribute it to increased levels of policing, as more money is spent on police today than ever.[9] Also, the American population is changing. Teenagers and young adults commit the most crimes, and today's generation of young people is relatively smaller than previous generations, e.g., the baby boomers.[10] This points to a controversial explanation offered by economists Steven Levitt and John Donahue, who link falling crime rates to abortion.[11] The legalization of abortion happened in the early 1970s, which meant there were fewer teenagers and young adults in the late 1980s and early 1990s—precisely when crime rates started to drop. As supporting evidence, they found that the five states that legalized abortion before *Roe v. Wade*—New York, California, Washington, Hawaii, and Alaska—all experienced earlier drops in crime. (Since its publication, both the substance and methods of this controversial study have been challenged by other scholars.)[12]

Since crime rates have dropped, surely Americans are less fearful of crime, right? Um, no. We actually think crime is getting worse. Gallup polls have regularly asked Americans if they thought there was more crime, less crime, or about the same amount of crime in their local area and the United States as a whole. As shown in Figure 7.2, over most of the last forty years, between a quarter and a half of Americans thought that crime was worsening in the area they lived. The percentage thinking the same about crime nationwide has varied, from a high of 90% to a low of 40%. In the most recent survey, one in two Americans think that crime is worsening where they live, and three in four feel that way about crime nationwide. (This difference in local versus national perceptions is another example of the optimism gap, as discussed in chapter 1.)

It's not easy to compare crime rates worldwide because countries

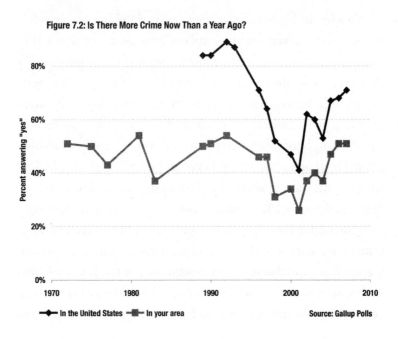

Figure 7.2: Is There More Crime Now Than a Year Ago?

Source: Gallup Polls

differ in how they define and measure crimes. Homicide is, again, probably the most reliable measure, and different regions of the world vary widely in their homicide rates. Australia and Europe have homicide rates one-third (or less) than that of the United States. The rest of North America and South America, on the other hand, have rates three times higher than the U.S.[13] Thirteen of the 15 countries with the highest homicide rates are in the Americas, headed by Honduras (61 homicides per 100,000), Jamaica (60), and Venezuela (52). This has been linked to gangs, organized crime, and, especially, the drug trade.[14] Among the safest countries in the world are those in Western Europe. Some European countries, such as Sweden, Norway, Iceland, and Spain, can't even get their homicide rate above 1 per 100,000.[15] If we rank all countries in the world, the United States comes in 51 out of 148 countries.[16]

Countries also vary in how they kill each other. About 60% of murders worldwide involve firearms.[17] Here in the Americas, we like to shoot each other. Three-fourths of murders in Central America involve guns, as do two-thirds of those in South America and half in North America. In Europe, Oceania, and Asia, however, fewer than 20% of murders involve firearms.[18] Not surprisingly, the regions with the most gun-related murders also have the most murders overall, though this correlation is difficult to interpret. Maybe guns make places dangerous, or dangerous places get more guns. Either way, the next time you fly to Europe, don't pack a gun in your carry-on. You probably won't need it.

If we go back in time, we find evidence that worldwide murder rates have dropped considerably over the centuries. Historians tell us that in the 1400s, the murder rate in Europe was as high as 35 murders per 100,000 people. From there it dropped rapidly for several centuries, through the 1700s, and dropped more slowly after that to its currently very low level of only 1 or 2 per 100,000 people. All told, the murder rate in Europe has dropped an astonishing

---

Christians Making a Difference

In 1965, John and Jan Gillespie invited a thirteen-year-old boy to their house for lunch after Sunday school. When he showed up with a packed suitcase, they realized he had run away from home. The boy ended up staying with them for a year and a half, and they felt a calling to help other young men like him. From this, John and Jan founded the Rawhide Boys Ranch in New London, Wisconsin. Located on a seven-hundred-acre parcel of land, its mission is to help troubled and delinquent boys. The Ranch has now grown to seven different homes, providing boys a place to live while they receive additional schooling, work experience, counseling, and moral training needed for them to successfully reintegrate into society. Many of the boys at Rawhide Ranch are referred there by the courts due to their delinquency, but a full three-quarters of them graduate from Rawhide Ranch and are not incarcerated again. Hundreds and hundreds of young men in the upper Midwest have been saved from a life of prison through the work of Rawhide Boys Ranch.[21]

90% over the past six centuries.[19] Historians explain this drop as a result from the government taking over the role of defense and justice. In the Middle Ages, people had to use personal violence to protect themselves and to right past wrongs. Over time, however, as governments became more powerful, they claimed a monopoly on violence. In turn, citizens have had to exert more self-control, letting the government administer justice.[20]

Prisoners

While we Americans are merely average when it come to shooting and robbing people, we excel at locking them up. Currently, 2.3 million adults are incarcerated in the United States—1.6 million in state and federal prisons and the rest in local jails.[22] Think about it: There are about 230 million adults in the United States, so 1 in 100 American adults are behind bars. If American prisoners were all in one place, it would be the fourth largest city in the United States, behind number-three Chicago (2.8 million) but ahead of

Houston (2.2 million people), and way ahead of Storrs, Connecticut (11,000 people). There are more prisoners nationwide than people living in each of fifteen states, including New Mexico, West Virginia, Nebraska, Idaho, and Maine. That's not all. The United States also has about another 5 million offenders under community supervision, such as probation or parole. This means that about 1 in 33 American adults are in the criminal justice system in some way or another.[23]

It hasn't always been this way. As shown in Figure 7.3, from the 1920s to the mid-1970s, our country had only about 100 prisoners for every 100,000 people—about 20% of the current imprisonment rate.[24] Starting in the mid-1970s, the incarceration rate shot up so fast that it doubled by 1985 and quadrupled by 1995.

Why do we put so many people in prison? Well, we know it's not because more people are committing crimes, for the crime rate actually fell during recent decades. Rather, we can credit (or blame)

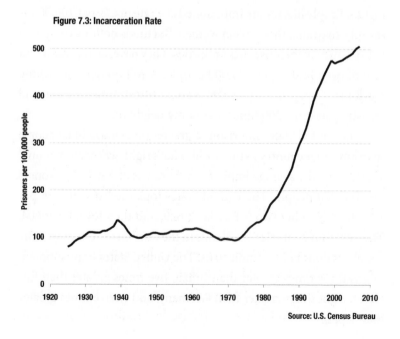

Figure 7.3: Incarceration Rate

Source: U.S. Census Bureau

various legal changes that "get tough on crime." The court systems now give longer sentences for common crimes, mandatory sentences for others, and reduced access to parole and probation.[25] Also, the government has put considerable money and effort into prosecuting drug offenses, including relatively minor ones. Currently, one-third of prisoners are in for drug offenses, compared to only 11% in 1970.[26]

We're also selective in whom we imprison. Men are ten times more likely than women to be imprisoned; blacks are six times more likely than whites; and Hispanics are twice as likely as whites.[27] Age also matters. Young adults in their twenties are more than twenty times as likely to be imprisoned as those over age fifty-five. Let's take these three factors—gender, race, and age—and put them together to illustrate the remarkable variation in who gets imprisoned in the United States. Our neighbor, a lovely woman, is white and over the age of fifty-five. Among older, white women like her, only 9 in 100,000 are imprisoned nationwide. I'm a white male in my late forties. People like me are imprisoned at a rate of 675 per 100,000—seventy-five times that of older women. But this is nothing compared to black men in their twenties or thirties. They have an imprisonment rate of over 11,000 per 100,000 people. A full one in nine young black men is in prison. This rate is about fifteen times my risk and an astronomical 1,200 times that of my neighbor.

The United States imprisons a greater percentage of its people than any other country in the world. That's right, we're number one! Worldwide, the average imprisonment rate is about 145 prisoners per 100,000 people. The United States tops the list with 756 per 100,000.[28] Number two is Russia, at 629, and then Rwanda at 604. The next four countries are islands in the Caribbean. Other wealthy countries don't hold a candle to us. The United States imprisonment rate is three times greater than Brazil, five times greater than England, eight times greater than Germany, and twelve times greater than Japan.

As you read this, perhaps you're wondering if you should care. After all, doesn't putting people in prison make society safer—and as long as it's not you who's in prison, why not? Certainly putting lots of people in prison lowers the crime rate, though it's difficult to know just how much. However, there are substantial costs associated with it as well. For starters, prisoners are very expensive. The state has to house, feed, clothe, and supervise them, and the yearly cost nationwide averages to about $24,000 per prisoner. Adding capital expenses—such as building and maintaining prisons—bumps this up to $65,000 per prisoner.[29] It's more expensive to put someone in prison than, say, to send them to college. Nearly $50 billion a year is spent on corrections; in many states it's one of the top budget items.[30] Guess who pays for this? (Hint: That person is holding this book.)

Imprisonment also creates havoc in people's lives. Besides the hardship of prison life itself, it makes problems in the broader community. People in prison can't properly raise their children or pay child support, which can create negative consequences for future generations. Prison life also teaches prisoners the skills and motivations for committing more crimes once they are released. Once they are freed, the stigma of imprisonment hinders their ability to reintegrate into society. A recent study found that employers contact job applicants with a prison record only 50% as often as those without a record—even if their job applications are otherwise identical.[31]

To be clear, I am not advocating that we empty our prisons. Certainly some people belong there. Rather, perhaps we have overlooked some of the considerable costs of imprisoning so many people. There may be an optimal rate of imprisonment. Going below this rate would unnecessarily increase crime rates, whereas going above it would pose too many costs on prisoners and society. I have no idea exactly where this ideal line is, but given the extraordinarily high imprisonment rate in the United States, it's a good bet we're above it.

Christians Making a Difference

Chuck Colson was a key member of President Nixon's administration, and in the wake of being indicted for his role in Watergate, he served seven months in prison on a separate charge. During this time, a friend gave him a copy of *Mere Christianity* by C. S. Lewis, and Colson became a born-again Christian. In the aftermath of his time in prison, Colson founded Prison Fellowship, a Christian prison ministry that brings justice and grace into the lives of prisoners. Prison Fellowship has programs both inside of prisons to educate and mentor prisoners, as well as outside of prisons to help prisoners reintegrate into society. But what many people know Prison Fellowship for is their Angel Tree Ministry. An estimated 1.7 million American children have a parent in prison, and Angel Tree seeks to show love to these children and reconcile them with their imprisoned parent. Angel Tree mobilizes churches to purchase, wrap, and deliver Christmas presents to these children on behalf of their imprisoned parent. These gifts are a powerful expression of love and grace for these children.[32]

Wars

Wars often feel arbitrary, as if they happen due to unique political and social circumstances, so we don't usually think about trends in warfare. Fortunately, some people have, and they have examined the severity of warfare in past decades. A good way of measuring the severity of a war is by calculating how many people wars have killed.[33] "Battle deaths" include all people who die in combat, both military and civilian. Obviously there were an extraordinary number of battle deaths in World War II, but what has happened since? As shown in Figure 7.4, the number of battle deaths worldwide has gone up and down in the past sixty-five years, but the overall trend is downward.[34] In the late 1940s and early 1950s, there were several costly wars, including the Chinese Civil War (1.2 million battle deaths), the Korean War (1.25 million deaths), the French-Indochina War (365,000 deaths), and the Greek Civil War (154,000 deaths). After that came the next big hump in the late 1960s with the Vietnam War (2.1 million). The 1980s saw both the Iraq-Iran

Figure 7.4: Worldwide Battle Deaths

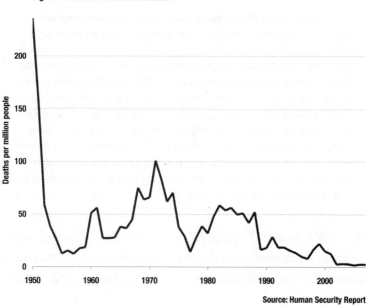

Source: Human Security Report

War (640,000) and the Soviet Invasion of Afghanistan (560,000). The overall death rate has dropped because the largest conflicts are becoming less severe—now killing hundreds of thousands of people rather than millions. If, however, we remove the large-scale conflicts from the data, the remaining smaller-scale conflicts produce a different picture. The battle deaths associated with them has fluctuated considerably since World War II, but the overall death rate has remained mostly steady.[35]

Racial Prejudice and Discrimination

Prejudice and discrimination can happen against just about any group, including those defined by age, ethnicity, gender, physical appearance, race, religion, or sexuality. For the purposes of this book, however, I will focus on racial and ethnic prejudice and discrimination. Racism casts a long, dark shadow on American history. While the Civil

Christians Making a Difference

As a teenager, Brad Phillips traveled around war-ravaged places with his father, allowing him to witness war and religious persecution at its worst—blood, starvation, disease, and death. This left a lasting impression on him, so in 1997, Brad launched a grassroots movement to mobilize American Christians to help the war victims in Sudan. This led to the founding of the Persecution Project Foundation, which operates out of a base camp in northern Kenya and has provided thousands of tons of humanitarian aid to the victims of genocide and religious persecution in Southern Sudan and Darfur. In addition, the Persecution Project Foundation has provided many other forms of assistance, including digging wells and building schools, churches, and health clinics—bringing life and health to one of the most violent, dangerous places on earth.[36]

War ended slavery 150 years ago, Jim Crow laws buttressed racism for another hundred years. Consider some of the race-based laws in force in different locales of the United States as recently as the 1960s.[37]

- Blacks and whites had to attend separate schools.
- They could not play pool or billiards together.
- They could not intermarry.
- They had to sit apart on buses and trains.
- They had to be kept apart in prisons.
- They had to sit in separate sections of the public library.
- White female nurses could not attend to black male patients.
- White baseball teams could not play near black playing fields.
- Black barbers could not cut the hair of white females.
- Students could not use textbooks first used by students of a different race.

There was even a movement to require African-Americans to pull aside for white drivers, allowing them to pass; it was eventually abandoned only because it was unworkable.[38]

Sociologists who study this issue focus on peoples' racially prejudiced attitudes. One level of racial prejudice—how citizens would feel about living in a neighborhood comprised predominately of members of another racial or ethnic group—has significantly declined in the past two decades. In 1990, 42% of white Americans "very much opposed" or "somewhat opposed" living in a mostly black neighborhood, but by the year 2008 this had dropped to 20%. Likewise, between 1990 and 2000, opposition to living with Asians, Hispanics, and Jews all dropped by at least 35%.

Tolerance and acceptance toward numerous racial and ethnic groups has increased. Between 1926 and 1997, sociologist Emory Borgardus and others measured college students' attitudes toward people from thirty different ancestral groups. They found increased acceptance toward all thirty groups, but, interestingly, the rank ordering of groups' acceptability did not change. Both in 1926 and in 1997, Northern Europeans were the most accepted groups, followed by Southern and Eastern Europeans. Mexicans, blacks, and Asians were among the least accepted groups.

Despite increasingly tolerant attitudes, racial discrimination still exists. Economists at the University of Chicago and MIT demonstrated this convincingly with a clever field experiment. They created two sets of fictitious résumés. One set had white-sounding names, such as "Emily Walsh" or "Greg Baker," and the other had African-American-sounding names, such as "Lakisha Washington" or "Jamal Jones." Otherwise the résumés were identical. They sent out thousands of these résumés, and they found that employers exhibited a marked preference for the "white" applicants, who received 1 callback for about every 10 applications. In contrast, the "black" applicants received only 1 callback for every 15 applications.[39]

It's somewhat difficult to compare prejudice levels worldwide, as different countries have different groups who are discriminated against. To get around this problem, the World Value Survey in 2005 asked people in fifty-three countries how they would feel about having "immigrants or foreign workers" as neighbors. In Figure 7.5, I summarize the responses from the twenty most populated countries. At the top of the list, the most intolerant country is Iran, among which 59% of respondents reported not wanting to live next to immigrants or foreign workers. Next are five Asian countries and France. The four most tolerant countries are in the western hemisphere: Argentina, Brazil, Mexico, and the U.S. Only 14% of Americans did not want foreign neighbors, suggesting that we rate fairly low in terms of outright xenophobia.

Freedom and Democracy

We Americans certainly value freedom. Think of the dirty looks you would get if you attended a political rally while holding up a sign calling for "less freedom now" or "end civil liberties." Beyond freedom

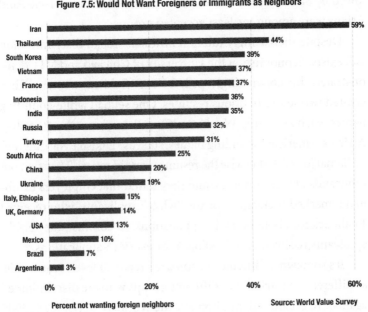

Figure 7.5: Would Not Want Foreigners or Immigrants as Neighbors

Percent not wanting foreign neighbors

Source: World Value Survey

being valued, it also associates with various forms of well-being.[40] Societies with greater freedom have happier citizens because they are allowed to make more choices about how they live.[41] Political freedom allows citizens to address the social problems of their society, and it associates with better physical health as well as fewer environmental problems.[42] Moreover, democratic accountability lessens political corruption.[43]

Every year, the research group Freedom House publishes a report on freedom in the world.[44] Using two dozen measures of political and civil liberties, it ranks countries into three categories: free, partly free, and not free. Free countries include most of Europe, Australia, New Zealand, Uruguay, Chile, Canada, and the United States. Partly free include Guatemala, Georgia, Honduras, Kenya, Kuwait, Lebanon, and Sri Lanka. The not-free club includes China, Cuba, Saudi Arabia, Libya, Somalia, Sudan, Uzbekistan, and North Korea.

Using Freedom House's ranking, we can track the freedom of countries worldwide. As shown in Figure 7.6, in 1990 only about 20% of the world's countries were ranked as free, and the rest were split between partly free and not free. Throughout the 1990s and 2000s, freedom came to Eastern Europe and other countries, such that now more than 45% of the world's countries are rated as free, and the partly free countries have dropped to 20%. If we measure freedom based on population rather than numbers of countries, we find similar numbers. In the mid-1990s, only about 20% of the world's population lived in free countries; now it's 45%.[45] Unfortunately, the percentage of not-free countries has remained fairly steady, at about 35%, indicating that freedom has come mostly to countries that were already partly free.

Reflecting this increased freedom, more countries are now democracies. In 1989, only about 40% of the world's countries (sixty-nine) were democracies, but now 60% (116) of them are. The total

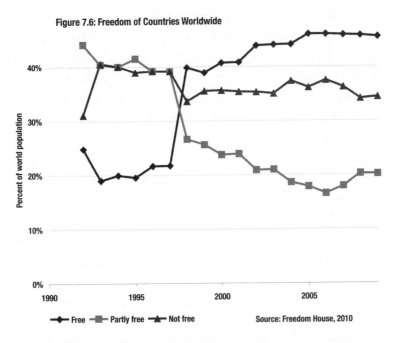

Figure 7.6: Freedom of Countries Worldwide

number of people living under democratic rule increased over the past century from 12% to 63%.[46] In 1900, no country in the world had universal adult suffrage, meaning that all adults could vote. Now the majority of countries have it.[47]

The Spread of Christianity

A commonly held myth is that Christianity is rapidly dying. Numerous articles and books have decried this apparent demise, some even asking if this is indeed the last Christian generation in America. I examined this issue in depth in my book *Christians are Hate-Filled Hypocrites . . . and Other Lies You've Been Told,* and here I present some data about the spread of Christianity, both in the United States and throughout the world.

Most Americans are Christians. A recent study by the Pew Foundation estimated that 3 out of 4 Americans affiliate with Christianity

Christians Making a Difference

Erik Hersman, a Christian, was raised in Kenya and Sudan by his American missionary parents. In 2007, the Kenyan national elections spawned violence throughout the country. In response, Erik and some friends created the Web site *www.ushahidi.com*, which allows people to report incidents of violence via text messages on their cell phone. The Web site then created a comprehensive crisis map, informing the world about both the amount and distribution of violence. This informs both governmental and international pressure to reduce the violence. Since then, Ushahidi has been used to monitor elections in India, track war violence in the Congo, and monitor rain forest destruction in Madagascar. It gives everyday people a voice about wrongdoing.[48]

to some degree.[49] Almost two-thirds of American Christians are Protestants, e.g., Evangelicals, Mainline Protestants, and those who attend historically black churches. Most of the remaining Christians are Roman Catholics.

About 16% of Americans do not affiliate with any religion; however, many of these unaffiliated people still have their own spiritual beliefs and practices. For example, a majority of the religiously unaffiliated believe in God or a higher power; in fact, only about 4% of all Americans are atheists (believing that God doesn't exist) or agnostics (believing that the existence of God cannot be known). The 8% or so of Americans who are neither Christian nor religiously unaffiliated adhere to other religions such as Judaism, Islam, Buddhism, and Hinduism.

Despite the fact that so many Americans today are Christians, many people assume that Americans were far more religious in the past. There are even Christian ministries devoted to returning America to the faith of its forefathers. This assumption about the past, however, doesn't stand up to scrutiny. Sociologists Roger Finke and Rodney Stark studied religious data dating back to Colonial times collected by the census, various religious denominations, and other sources. They found that Americans have become progressively more religious over the centuries.[50] By their estimation, fewer than 20% of Americans in the 1700s adhered to a religion (almost always Christianity), and throughout the 1800s, levels of adherence steadily increased until by the end of the century they were about 50%. In the 1900s, adherence rates rose even more, going from 50% to over 60%. In this light, the last fifty years of American history might well constitute its most religious period yet.

Over the past twenty years, however, another trend has surfaced in American religion—the rise of religious unaffiliation. In the 1970s and 1980s, few Americans, only 6% to 8%, did not affiliate with any religion, but this percentage doubled in the 1990s, so that now about 16% to 18% of Americans are religiously unaffiliated. Nonetheless, over the past twenty years, the percentage of Americans affiliating with Catholicism and Evangelical churches has remained roughly stable; it is affiliation with mainline Protestant churches that has dropped precipitously.

Worldwide, an estimated 33% of all people are Christian, followed by 20% Muslim, 15% nonreligious or atheist, 13% Hindu, 6% traditional Chinese folk religions, 5% Buddhist, and the rest aligning with other, smaller religions.[51] The region with the highest concentration of Christians is Latin America, where 93% of the people adhere to the Christian faith. North America, Oceania, and Europe are not far behind, with Christian populations ranging from 77% to 84% of the population. Forty-five percent of Africans are Christians, as are 9% of people living in Asia.[52]

Christianity and Islam are the two fastest-growing religions in terms of absolute numbers. Every new day sees an additional 70,000 or so Christians in the world, and about an equal number of new Muslims.[53] The same twenty-four-hour time period also witnesses increases in the number of Hindus (37,000), the non-religious and atheists (18,000), and Chinese folk-religionists and Buddhists (about 10,000 each). While Christianity is often characterized as a Western

---

Christians Making a Difference

The Bible is at the heart of Christianity, so it's difficult for a people group to encounter Christianity fully if it doesn't have a Bible translation in its own language. Wycliffe Bible Translators International plays a significant role in this regard. Founded in 1942, Wycliffe aims to translate the Bible into every language on earth. To appreciate the need for their work, there are nearly 6,900 languages currently being used in the world, and two thousand of them—representing a billion people—do not have the New or Old Testament translated into their language. Many of these languages without Bibles are found in Papua New Guinea and Indonesia, Southeast and Central Asia, and Central Africa. Wycliffe has contributed to seven hundred completed translations so far, and it is currently working on fifteen hundred more. Bible translators are highly committed, for it takes ten to twenty years to translate the New Testament into a new language.[55]

---

religion, its greatest growth is elsewhere. Africa sees 25,000 new Christians each day. Latin America and Asia see about 20,000 new Christians, and North America and Europe lag behind, at 5,000 and about 2,000 respectively.[54]

The Danger of Thinking the World Is a Dangerous Place

Chapter 1 detailed some of the problems associated with excessive pessimism, including anxiety and health problems. Overestimating how dangerous the world is also leads to a general distrust of the people and places around us. This chapter highlights many things for which we can be thankful. Crime rates have fallen considerably, even for the most serious crimes. The world's population now has fewer war deaths and more freedom, and the number of Christians grows every day. Even racial prejudice is diminishing. These are things for which we can rejoice and be glad. Not only are these good feelings an accurate response to the world's situation, they are also good for us.

CHAPTER 8

WHAT ABOUT MARRIAGE AND FAMILIES?

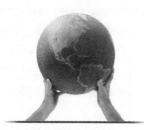

Slightly more than 40% of contemporary first marriages are likely to end in divorce.

—*W. Bradley Wilcox, sociologist*[1]

Premarital sex is normal behavior for the vast majority of Americans, and has been for decades.

—*Lawrence Finer, Guttmacher Institute*[2]

We need to rebuild the family. . . . The future of our land depends in large part on the strength of our families.

—*Sam Brownback, republican senator from Kansas*[3]

Many of today's moral debates center on marriage and the family. From the perspective of many Christians, if there's one topic that demonstrates that the world isn't what it used to be, it's the collapse of families. We hear a lot about high divorce rates, children born out of wedlock, and abortion. To some extent, the pessimists are right. Some of these issues indeed pose problems for our society, and we should not gloss over them. Nonetheless, it's still important to separate the legitimately bad news from the hype. Are family and marriage issues really getting worse? Was there ever really a "good ol' days" for families? In this chapter, I explore these questions.

Divorce

This year my wife and I celebrate our twentieth anniversary. When we made it to our fifth anniversary, my father told us that we had made it longer than half the marriages in California, where he lived. He was joking, but he wasn't off by much. How many marriages in America end in divorce? A lot. Demographers estimate that one-third of all first marriages end in divorce, separation, or annulment in their first ten years, and about 40% to 50% end in the first twenty years.[4]

This high divorce rate is bad news because divorce is associated with many problems.[5] Compared to married people, divorced people have higher rates of alcoholism, smoke more, have more health problems, are more socially isolated, experience more negative events, and have higher levels of depression. They also have lower earnings, less satisfying sex lives, less happiness, and less self-acceptance.[6] Divorced people even have shorter lives. Biologist Harold Morowitz observed that being a divorced non-smoker is only slightly less dangerous than being a pack-a-day married person. He quipped that "if a man's marriage is driving him to heavy smoking, he has a delicate decision to make."[7]

Divorce corresponds with problems for children as well. Compared to children from intact houses, children with divorced parents are twice as likely to drop out of high school. Girls are three times more likely to become teen mothers, and boys twice as likely to spend time in prison.[8] Sociologist Paul Amato gauges the impact of high divorce rates on our society by estimating how our nation would be different if families today were as intact as they were in 1960. He calculates that if divorce rates and other family disruptions today were as low as they were fifty years ago, we would have 70,000 fewer suicides, 500,000 fewer acts of teen delinquency, 600,000 fewer children receiving therapy, and 750,000 fewer children repeating a grade.[9]

Granted, some marriages are sufficiently violent, both physically and emotionally, that divorce may be in the children's best interest; in fact, studies have found that children actually do better when marriages characterized by domestic abuse or screaming matches end in divorce.[10] However, most divorces, maybe two-thirds, do not result from violence; instead, they are caused by couples simply growing apart. These types of divorces are particularly traumatic for children. W. Bradley Wilcox, a sociologist who heads the National Marriage Project, summarizes their effect by concluding that "the clear majority of divorces involving children in America are not in the best interests of the children."[11]

But there is a bit of good news here. Believe it or not, divorce rates have actually steadily fallen over the past thirty years. As shown in Figure 8.1, the divorce rate climbed slowly but steadily from 1920 to 1960 with one big exception—a jump in 1946 due to the dissolution of wartime marriages. Starting in 1960, however, the divorce rate started to skyrocket, more than doubling in the next two decades. At its peak in 1979, there were 22.8 divorces each year for every 1,000 marriages. Since then the divorce rate has declined, and now it's at 16.4—about a 30% drop.[12]

The divorce rate grew in the last century for both economic and legal reasons. More women were employed, which allowed them to take care of themselves and their children after a divorce, if need be.[13] Employment also led to friendships with other potential partners as well as exposing women to new ideas and greater independence.[14] From a legal perspective, the 1970s saw the introduction of no-fault

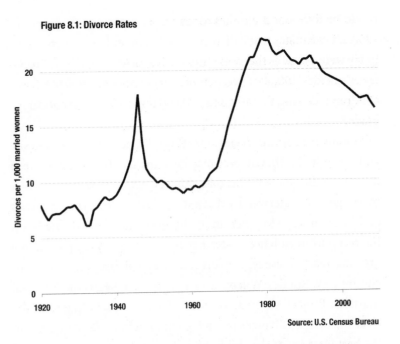

Figure 8.1: Divorce Rates

Source: U.S. Census Bureau

divorces. Previously, couples wanting to divorce needed to demonstrate a wrong, such as adultery, extreme cruelty, desertion, or time in prison. No-fault divorce, however, provided more easily met criteria, such as incompatibility or irreconcilable differences.[15] Along with these changes came more acceptance and less social stigma toward divorce.[16]

The divorce rate has declined in recent decades due to various demographic changes. Americans are getting married later in life: The median age of marriage for women in 1960 was about 23 years old, and now it's 26. For men the median age has gone from about 23 years to more than 27.[17] Couples who marry later tend to be more stable both in their lives and careers, and they form longer-lasting marriages. Americans are better educated, and education correlates with longer-lasting marriages.[18] Also, as the baby-boomer generation has gotten older (but don't tell them—it upsets them), there are relatively fewer Americans in their twenties through forties—the peak age range for divorces.[19]

As you might expect, divorce is not random; some types of people are more likely to get divorced than others. In a large-scale study of women, The National Survey of Family Growth collected data on 10,000 women starting in the year 1973, and it identified which married women were most likely to get divorced. As shown in Figure 8.2, divorce rates were associated with various economic, social, and psychological factors.[20] As a baseline, 43% of the women in the study married but got divorced or separated within fifteen years of their marriage. At the high end of divorce rates, 65% of women from poorer families got divorced or separated. Likewise, 50% of women who were not employed got divorced. High divorce rates were also observed among women who grew up in broken homes (52%) and in couples who lived together before marriage (50%). Women who had previously been raped had high divorce

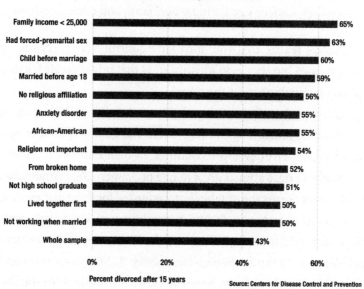

Figure 8.2: Women Most Likely to Get Divorced

Category	Percent divorced after 15 years
Family income < 25,000	65%
Had forced-premarital sex	63%
Child before marriage	60%
Married before age 18	59%
No religious affiliation	56%
Anxiety disorder	55%
African-American	55%
Religion not important	54%
From broken home	52%
Not high school graduate	51%
Lived together first	50%
Not working when married	50%
Whole sample	43%

Percent divorced after 15 years

Source: Centers for Disease Control and Prevention

161

rates (63%) as did women with anxiety disorders (55%). Finally, women who were not affiliated with any religion had high divorce rates (56%).

But let's take a moment to focus on the positive. If we turn the question of divorce around, we can ask what kinds of marriages generally stay together. Social psychologist David Myers compiled this list of factors associated with marital success.[21] To have a long-lasting, stable marriage, you should:

- get married after age twenty;
- grow up in a stable, two-parent household;
- date for a while before marriage—don't rush into it;
- get a good education;
- earn a stable income from a good job;
- do not live together before marriage;
- do not have sex before marriage;
- be religiously committed and worship together;
- marry someone of a similar age, faith, and education level.

Now, I realize that you don't have control over every one of these factors, but they help identify areas that might create friction for you if you don't meet the criteria.

Compared to other developed countries, the United States excels at getting divorced. The United Nations has gathered divorce-rate data for thirty-five developed countries. By their estimation, Americans have a crude annual divorce rate of 3.7 per 1,000 Americans. (*Crude* here means the number is not adjusted for the marriage rate, as opposed to how people act.) Several Eastern European countries, such as Lithuania, Latvia, and the Czech Republic, are right behind us with crude divorce rates above 3. Most European and other developed countries have rates between 2 and 3. At the low end are traditionally Catholic countries, such as Ireland, Italy, and Mexico, which have divorce rates of .7 or .8.[22]

Why does the U.S. have such a high divorce rate? A study of international students attending college in the United States suggests an intriguing possibility.[23] Psychologists interviewed students from India, Pakistan, Thailand, Mexico, Brazil, Japan, Hong Kong, the Philippines, Australia, England, and the United States. The researchers asked these students to rate the importance of romantic love for starting and sustaining a marriage. Overall, students from the Western countries—the countries with the highest divorce rates—put the highest premium on romantic love. This suggests the possibility that marriages based on romance struggle when the passion inevitably simmers down. Now, if this is true, I'm not sure what its practical implications are. Perhaps we should put up billboards proclaiming that romance is overrated?

Christians Making a Difference

Bob and Audrey Meisner are not just Christians—they are visible, influential Christians. They co-host the Canadian television ministry *It's a New Day*, which is shown throughout Canada and the northern United States. After years of marriage, Bob and Audrey gave every indication of "having it all"—three beautiful children, exciting jobs, and a committed marriage. At this point, however, Audrey's friendship with another man turned into an emotional affair, which led to adultery. Not only that, she became pregnant with the other man's child. Bob was utterly devastated when he found out, and he faced a choice about his marriage and the child. He chose to embrace them both, and to do whatever was necessary to restore his relationship with Audrey, including counseling, mentoring, and ultimately moving to a new location to refocus their lives. Bob even gave the child his own name—Robert—and the child's middle name is Theodore, meaning "gift of God." Bob and Audrey used this crisis not only to reaffirm the centrality of marriage in their own lives but also to encourage thousands of other couples to build, protect, and value their marriage.[24]

Single-Parent Families

Single-parent families are sometimes the by-product of divorce. Children from single-parent families have more negative experiences than those from two-parent families.[25] For example, over half of single-parent children, 59%, live below the poverty line, compared to only 13% of children living with both parents.[26] Single-parent children also drop out of school more often, act more aggressively, and are more sexually active.[27] Single-parent children are more likely to abuse alcohol and drugs[28] and are arrested more often. In one study, teenagers who lived without their fathers were three times more likely to be incarcerated at some point in their lives than those who lived with fathers.[29] Overall, children from single-parent families are generally less happy than those from intact families.[30] The impact of being raised in a single-parent family is summarized by sociologist Sara McLanahan, a leading scholar in the area and herself a single mom for ten years. She writes: "When I first got into this research, I wanted to demonstrate that single mothers could do just as good a job of raising children as married moms. Unfortunately, the evidence led me to somewhat different conclusions."[31]

To be clear, this does not imply that single parents are not good parents. Quite the contrary, some of the single parents that I know amaze me with the time, effort, skill, and love they give their children. They are outstanding parents, but there is only one of them. This means that they simply have less to give their children: less discipline, less physical care, and less emotional support.[32] I've experienced this in brief when my wife has taken one- or two-week trips to visit family. At first the change in routine is fun for me and the boys (think mice playing when cat is away), but in a few days we're all pretty miserable. On my wife's last trip, I put my nine-year-old son into bed way too late for a school night, and he gently reminded me, "Dad, you forgot to make dinner." So, down we went to the kitchen for fried eggs and bacon. After about two days alone, I start shaking my head, wondering how single parents do it.

Unfortunately, the number of children raised without both parents in the house is quite high. Currently, 30% of American children live without both parents; the majority of them live with their mother only.[33] As shown in Figure 8.3, in 1960 only 12% of children did not live with both of their parents, but this number rose dramatically over the next several decades until it hit 32% in 1995—a 250% increase! Since 1995, the rate of single-parented children has leveled off and even dropped a percentage point or two.

The rise in single-parent families has resulted, in part, from Americans getting married at an older age. Relative to 1960, we now get married later in life, in our late twenties rather than early twenties.[34] However, women still have children in their late teens and early twenties, meaning there are more children born into unwed circumstances. In 1960, only 5% of children were born into

Figure 8.3: Children Living Without Both Parents

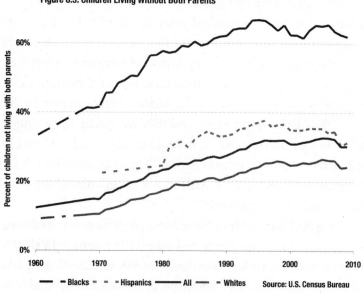

165

a household without two married parents. By 2005 it was 37%, and there is no sign of this trend slowing down.[35] It's also now more acceptable to have children outside of marriage.[36] A recent survey found that 52% of Americans thought that it was "never" or only "sometimes" wrong, compared to 44% who viewed it as "usually" or "always" wrong.[37]

Hidden in these national trends are enormous race and ethnic differences in single-parent families. Whereas 24% of white children live without two parents in the house, 32% of Hispanic children do, and a remarkable 62% of African-American children do—two-and-a-half times that of white children. The majority of African-American children, 69%, are born out of wedlock. Sociologists Claude Fischer and Douglas Hout correctly label this race difference in family experiences "a major story of the twentieth century."[38]

Why do so few African-American children have both parents at home? Some scholars trace this problem back to slavery and its destabilization of family life, but this doesn't explain why the racial gap started to widen a hundred years after the Civil War. A more promising explanation points to the shortage of marriageable black men. Starting in the 1960s, many African-American men lost their good-paying, industrialized jobs as these jobs left American cities. In addition, as covered previously, African-American men are far more likely to be imprisoned, and they die earlier. If we simply define being "marriageable" as having a good job and not being in prison, then there are far fewer African-American men available for marriage. As a consequence, African-American women have more children outside of marriage.[39]

Since the United States ranks number one in divorce rates among industrialized nations, I expected more of the same with single-parent families, but it turns out that we're only middle-of-the-pack; the Scandinavian countries dominate. In Sweden, for example, 55%

Christians Making a Difference

Love INC is a Christian organization that guides local churches in recognizing and meeting the needs in their communities. It describes itself as "a movement of Christian churches working together to show God's love to the poor and needy." Started in 1977, and now headquartered in Minneapolis, it represents a network of over nine thousand churches, and in the year 2009, it was responding to over three thousand calls a day for help nationwide. One of these calls came from Sarah, an eighteen-year-old single mother. Love INC put Sarah in touch with members of local churches in Oregon City, Oregon, and a volunteer delivered a crib for Sarah's baby. In doing so, she noticed that Sarah had many other needs. Ultimately, various churches came together to provide Sarah furniture, clothing, dishes, toys, and a new car seat. Several local churches even collected a donation for Sarah. Through efforts like these, Love INC has helped countless thousands of people in need.[41]

---

of children live without both parents. Even France and England average 40%. At the other end of the spectrum, Germany weighs in at 20%, Italy at 9%, and Japan at only 1%.[40]

Marital Happiness and Family Time

So far in this chapter I have focused on the structure of American families, but now let's turn to their quality. To start with, are people happy with their marriages? Since 1973, the General Social Survey has asked married respondents the following question: "Taking things all together, how would you describe your marriage? Would you say that your marriage is very happy, pretty happy, or not too happy?" As shown in Figure 8.4, most married people are relatively happy with their marriage. Currently, a little over 60% report being very happy, 35% are pretty happy, and a few are not too happy. Looking back in time, the percentage of respondents who were very happy was highest from the early 1970s to the mid-1980s, at which point it dropped a bit and has stayed at this level since.

There is, of course, interplay between marital happiness and

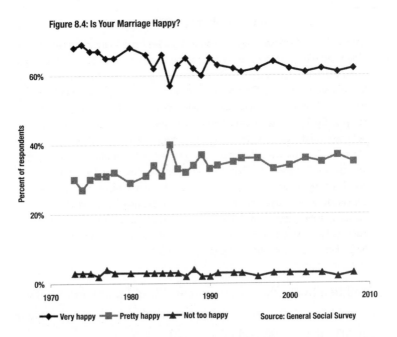

Figure 8.4: Is Your Marriage Happy?

◆ Very happy ■ Pretty happy ▲ Not too happy   Source: General Social Survey

divorce. The low number of not-very-happy marriages might simply reflect the dissolution of the least happy marriages. Ironically, the high divorce rate in our nation may ensure that the remaining marriages are relatively happy. In support of this interpretation, the slight bump downward in marital happiness happened at about the same time the divorce rate started dropping. So it could be that the drop in the divorce rate resulted from more people staying in fairly happy (but not very happy) marriages.

Turning to family life, let's focus on how much time parents spend with their children. Not that all parent-child time is quality time, but studies have found that time with parents positively affects children's development.[42] For example, adolescents who spend time with and feel close to a parent are less prone to smoking, drinking, doing drugs, being involved in sexual activity, and having suicidal thoughts. They also get better grades and are more likely to go to college.[43]

Data from long-term studies suggest that parent-child time is on the rise. A sociological study conducted in Muncie, Indiana, in 1924, found that 60% of fathers spent at least one hour a day with their children. This rose to 81% in 1977 and 83% in 1999. Similarly, in 1924, only 45% of mothers spent two or more hours with their children, compared to 65% in 1977 and 71% in 1999.[44] More recently, national time diary studies using different measures have found a similar pattern of increasing time with children. Married fathers in 1965 and 1975 averaged only 17 minutes a day interacting with their children. By 1985 this was 26 minutes, and by 1999 it nearly doubled—to 51 minutes a day. Mothers showed a somewhat different pattern. In 1965 all mothers, whether married or single, averaged 80 minutes a day with their children. This actually dropped to 65 minutes in 1975, but then it started climbing. By 1999 it was 95 minutes a day.[45] Parents in 2006 spent more time talking, playing with, and praising their children than they did in 1998.[46] This increase might be unexpected since more women work outside of the home and there are more single-parent families.

Why are parents spending more time with their children? Several causes have been suggested. One big importance is that, due to widespread birth control, childbearing is now more voluntary, so adults who have children are more likely to want them and be committed to them. Also, family sizes are smaller, leaving more parental time for each child. Finally, parents keep children closer to home now than in the past due to safety concerns (real or imagined, as we saw from a previous chapter). Years ago, parents often let their children out of the house, unsupervised for much of the day. Today, parents monitor their children much more closely, so there are fewer free-range kids running around. I've witnessed this change in my own family. My father tells me that when he was a kid, he would take off with his friends in the morning and the sole expectation was that he would be back by dinner. When I was a little guy, I would routinely walk to friends' houses or to the store, even if it was a mile or two away. (I also had to walk to school backwards in snow, but that's a different story.) My kids, however, are not allowed to walk off our street until they get into middle school, and my seventeen-year-old didn't get complete freedom of movement until he got his driver's license.[47]

We're not the only country to witness more parenting time. A study of sixteen industrialized countries, including Australia, Belgium, Finland, Germany, Hungary, Italy, Norway, and the United Kingdom, found a similar increase.[48] In 1960, fathers of young children in these countries spent an average of twenty-four minutes a day with their kids, but by 2000 it was up to an hour and twelve minutes. Both working mothers and stay-at-home mothers increased their time with children by over an hour. While mothers still spend more time with their kids than do fathers, the gap has been closing over time.

Cohabitation

Cohabitation, or living together, has become increasingly popular.[49] According to a nationwide study, in 2007, 9% of people ages 15 to 44 were cohabitating with someone.[50] Thirty-six percent of all adults have cohabited at some time in their lives.[51] This number is higher among younger adults, of whom it is estimated that slightly more than half will cohabitate at some point in their lives.[52]

Cohabitation can be a rather short-lived experience: About 55% of cohabitating couples marry within five years, while 40% break up.[53] Cohabitation has become much more common over the past forty years. In 1970, only 1% of couples lived together, but by 1999 it had increased to over 7%.[54] In the early 1970s, only about 10% of marriages started out with cohabitation, but now it's over 50%.[55]

Today, many people believe that living together is a good way to decide whether marriage is for them, but despite its popularity, cohabitation is associated with undesirable outcomes. Once they marry, couples who cohabitated first end up scoring lower on measures of marital quality, and they get divorced more frequently—a statistic most people don't seem to realize.[56] A 2008 survey asked Americans if they thought that couples living together before marriage would be more or less likely to get divorced than couples who did not. Forty-nine percent of respondents thought that cohabitating couples got divorced less often, and only 31% correctly answered that they got divorced more often.[57]

The link between cohabitation and weaker marriages can be explained in different ways. Perhaps the type of people who live together first are also those who shy away from long-term commitment, or maybe they have nontraditional values or even poor relationship skills. If so, they might be at high risk for divorce whether or not they live together first. On the other hand, cohabitation may weaken later marriage by signifying it as less important and casting the relationship as something that is easily ended.[58] Whatever the case, there is little evidence that cohabitation actually improves the quality of later marriage.

Why are more couples living together? Society is much less disapproving of cohabitation now than it was in times past. Throughout much of the twentieth century, it was actually illegal in various locales for a couple to live together if they weren't married, and laws allowed landlords and hotels to refuse unmarried couples. This is not to say, however, that living together is a new idea. In the 1920s, there was a short-lived movement for "trial marriages." It argued that couples should try living together for a defined period of time, and if it worked out, the couple could formally marry.[59]

To many people, the issue of cohabitation is a question of whether or not sex outside of marriage is morally acceptable. Sexuality in general is an area of strong contention in our society and well worth a closer look.

Sex and Sexuality

I suppose if there's one thing that most people think is getting worse over time, it has to be sexual misconduct. Have you turned on the television lately or flipped through a magazine? Case closed, right? Actually, when we look at the data, it's more of a mixed story.

Starting with premarital sex, parents have good reason to be concerned about their children's sexual activity. Early sexual activity is linked to emotional and physical health risks including sexually transmitted diseases and pregnancies.[60] Also, women who have pre-marital sex are more likely to get divorced once they marry.[61] It turns out, however, that high school students are somewhat less sexually active now than in the near past. As shown in Figure 8.5, 39% of ninth-graders in 1991 had had sexual intercourse, and now it's down to 32%. Likewise, it dropped for sophomores (48% to 41%), juniors (62% to 53%), and seniors (67% to 62%). All told, currently a little under half (46%) of high school students have had sexual intercourse.

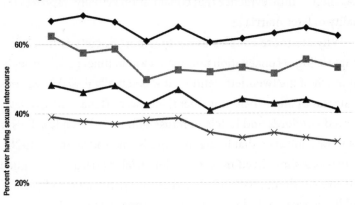

Figure 8.5: Sexual Intercourse Rates Among High School Students

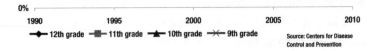

Source: Centers for Disease Control and Prevention

Among adults, however, premarital sex is ubiquitous, and it's been this way for a while. Figure 8.6 plots the sexual histories of three generations of people; those currently ages 15 to 25, ages 35 to 45, and ages 55 to 65.[62] For simplicity, I'll refer to these generations as young people, parents, and grandparents. Figure 8.6 shows how many people of each generation had premarital sex by a given age. For example, 74% of today's young people have had premarital sex by age 20 compared with 72% of parents and 48% of grandparents. You'll notice that all three curves, those for young people, parents, and grandparents, get pretty high. Eventually, 93% of people in the parents' generation had premarital sex as did 88% of the grandparents. Gramps, Grandma, what's up with that? Basically, premarital sex is a near-universal experience for Americans, and it has been for some time now.

We're not the first generation of parents to worry about the

Figure 8.6: Premarital Sex Rates by Generation

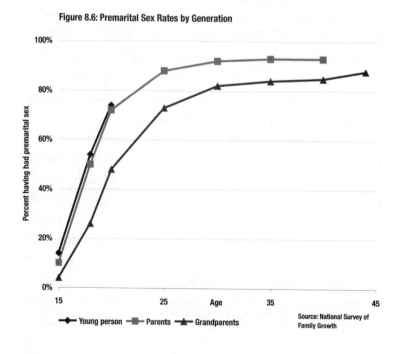

Source: National Survey of Family Growth

sexual behavior of our children. A 1929 study conducted in Muncie, Indiana, found mothers decrying the sexual morals of their children.[63] Mothers of teenage boys, especially, complained about the fast and loose girls of that time (who, by the way, are in their late nineties now). Apparently, these girls were far too aggressive; they would call boys up and make dates and dress in a scandalous fashion. Researchers even heard that the previous summer, six girls organized a party and invited six boys, and no one got home until three in the morning!

For people already married, premarital sex is no longer an option, so sexual misconduct might take the form of extramarital sex. The General Social Survey asked married respondents if they had ever had sex with someone who was not their spouse. Of the respondents asked this question since the year 2000, 18% of those who had ever been married reported straying from their marriage.[64]

Depending on your expectations, this percentage of married people who have ever cheated in their marriage may be high or low. However, married people are clearly less likely to sleep around than non-marrieds. A nationwide study in 2002 found that only 4.5% of currently married men ages 15 to 44 had more than one female sexual partner in the last twelve months, compared to 30.5% of the men who had never married nor were cohabiting. Likewise, only 3.8% of married women had multiple, male sexual partners in the previous year, compared to 24% of never-married, not-cohabitating women.[65]

Whether Americans approve of non-marital sex depends on who does it. Figure 8.7 presents data from the General Social Survey, and as shown, Americans have increasingly negative attitudes toward extramarital sex. In the 1970s, about 70% of respondents deemed extramarital sex to be always wrong, but now it's over 80%. Likewise, most Americans condemn teen sex (kids ages 14 to 16) as always wrong. In contrast, Americans have become more accepting of premarital sex, with only about one-quarter viewing it as always wrong. The greatest change in attitude, however, regards gay sex. Through about 1990, three-quarters of Americans condemned it as wrong, but now only about half do.

Abortions

Abortion raises many legal and moral issues, but here I will simply describe the prevalence of abortions. Every year, about 2% of all women between ages 15 and 44 have an abortion, and over their life-span, nearly one-third of all women will have had an abortion.[66] Currently, the rate of abortion is 23 abortions for every 100 live births. This rate has fluctuated since the legalization of abortion in 1973. As shown in Figure 8.8, the abortion rate increased through 1980, when it peaked at 36 abortions per 100 live births. Since then it has dropped fairly steadily so that it is now down to 23 abortions per 100 live births.[67]

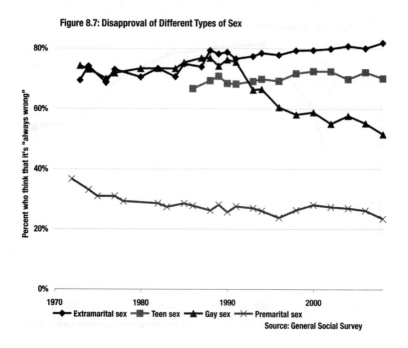

Figure 8.7: Disapproval of Different Types of Sex

Percent who think that it's "always wrong"

Extramarital sex — Teen sex — Gay sex — Premarital sex

Source: General Social Survey

175

Women vary in their likelihood of getting abortions. Girls under the age of fifteen years are the most likely to terminate a pregnancy—with a rate of 76 abortions for every 100 live births. Unmarried women and African-Americans also have high rates, at 49 and 47 respectively. Caucasian women are least likely to have abortions—with a rate of 16 abortions per 100 live births. Women in their early thirties stand at 14 abortions, and married women statistically have 6 abortions per 100 live births. Women living below the poverty level have substantially higher abortion rates, as do women who do not affiliate with a religion.[68]

Attitudes toward abortion have followed the same track as its prevalence. Americans' acceptance of unrestricted abortion (abortions with no legal limitations) increased from the 1960s through the mid-1970s, but since then has slowly declined.[69] In a recent CBS News Poll, 36% of Americans supported unrestricted access to

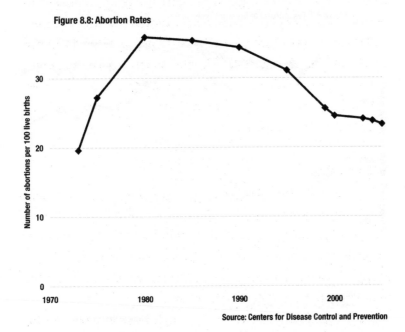

Figure 8.8: Abortion Rates

Number of abortions per 100 live births

Source: Centers for Disease Control and Prevention

Christians Making a Difference

Unplanned pregnancies can make for excruciatingly difficult decisions. Adoption by Choice, a private Christian nonprofit organization in Erie, Pennsylvania, supports women in this situation, helping them consider the benefits of adoption. This organization makes adoption as comfortable and viable as possible. It offers free counseling and prenatal care, as well as assistance in obtaining medical and legal services. The birth mother can choose the adopting family, and she can request letters and photos of her child throughout its childhood. This innovative approach has supported many young women during their unplanned pregnancy and helped them to appreciate the value of adoption.[73]

---

abortion, 39% supported restricted access, and 23% thought abortions should not be permitted.[70] The people most in support of abortion are those with college educations as well as those living in the Northeastern United States and the West Coast.[71]

Worldwide, the abortion rate has fallen over the last couple of decades.[72] In 1995, the worldwide abortion rate was estimated to be 35 abortions for every 1,000 women between the ages of 15 and 44. This dropped to 29 by the year 2003—a nearly 20% reduction in just eight years. Abortion rates fell considerably in Eastern Europe, and they fell somewhat in Latin America, Asia, and Africa. They remained stable in Western Europe. Currently, an estimated 1 in 5 pregnancies end in abortion.

A Mixed Bag

So in the areas of marriage, family, and sexuality, are things improving or getting worse? It depends where you look. Parents are spending more time with their children than they did even a decade or two ago, but the U.S. has more divorces and single-parent households than it did a century ago, even though the trends of both have leveled off if not dropped somewhat in recent decades. Premarital sex rates are very high, but they have been for some time. Abortion rates both here and abroad have dropped in recent decades.

All in all, this is certainly not a "three cheers for us!" chapter. That said, there is no evidence that we are in a downward spiral that dissolves all morality in society. The world is truly a complex place and, especially with family and sexual issues, one-sided headlines and blustery talking points can't begin to capture what's really going on.

CHAPTER 9

WHAT ABOUT THE ENVIRONMENT?

On a shelf in my office is a small pile of recent books about the environment which I plan to reread obsessively if I'm ever found to have a terminal illness, because they are so unsettling that they may make me less upset about being snatched from life in my prime.

—*David Owen,* New Yorker *magazine*[1]

You have to admit the environment is getting better, not worse.
—*Terry Anderson, director of the Property and Environment Research Center*[2]

Future generations may well have occasion to ask themselves, "What were our parents thinking [about the environment]? Why didn't they wake up when they had the chance?"
—*Al Gore,* An Inconvenient Truth

Let me start this chapter with a caveat. I am a sociologist, not a physical scientist, so any technical discussion of the environment is instantly out of my league. I wouldn't know carcinogenic polycyclic hydrocarbon (a type of pollutant found in fossil fuels) if I stepped in it. Do you want to understand the chemical reactions underpinning global warming? Put this book down and keep moving down the bookshelf.

As such, my discussion of the environment will focus on basic issues: Is the air and water getting cleaner or dirtier? Are we losing forests? These questions are easier to answer than you might think because most important environmental data is collected by governments and multinational organizations who make the data available to the public.[3] Consequently, a non-expert, such as me, can work with the same facts as the experts.

How We Think About the Environment

Most statements on the environment have a clear message: The world is in trouble—a lot of trouble. We've heard this message for some time now. In 1991, then senate majority leader, George Mitchell, described the impending ecological disaster. He stated that they "are killing our water, our air, our plants, our animals, and eventually, if not checked, they will kill us." If not halted, "life as we know it will change dramatically in the twenty-first century, and much of it will end."[4] A children's book about the environment describes the situation in no uncertain terms. "The balance of nature is delicate but essential for life. Humans have upset that balance, stripping the land of its green cover, choking the air, poisoning the sea."[5] The environmental group Worldwatch Institute writes that "depending on the degree of misery and biological impoverishment that we are prepared to accept, we have only one or perhaps two generations in which to reinvent ourselves."[6] *Time* magazine summarized the conventional wisdom: "Everyone knows that the planet is in bad shape."[7]

Some of these apocalyptic messages appear to be strategic in nature. Environmental groups, mostly nonprofits, rely on donations, and they use alarmism both to convey their message and to acquire resources. For example, after writing the last sentence, I pulled up the home page for the environmental group Greenpeace, and the lead story boldly proclaimed that "Two-thirds of polar bears will be dead by 2050." (I assume they mean the population size of polar bears will drop two-thirds, not that two-thirds of the bears alive today will die in the next four decades. Polar-bear longevity seems a less stirring issue.) Other headlines lament the loss of the Indonesian rain forest, a dirty coal plant in Massachusetts, and the impact of the British Petroleum Deepwater Horizon oil spill. Mixed in with these fear messages are appeals for help, especially donations. Halfway down the Web page is a photograph of a handsome young person climbing a rock, and the accompanying text proclaims: "Donate today. We are independent and rely on people like YOU who make our work possible. DONATE."

A while ago, Greenpeace mistakenly posted on its Web site an incomplete draft of a press release. It read: "In the twenty years since the Chernobyl tragedy, the world's worst nuclear accident, there have been nearly (FILL IN ALARMIST AND ARMAGED-DONIST FACTOID HERE)."[8] This press release template illustrates the strategic role of alarmism in the work of environmental groups. In fact, a Greenpeace activist has observed that "the truth is that many environmental issues we fought for ten years back are as good as solved. Even so, the strategy continues to focus on the assumption that 'everything is going to hell.'"[9] I understand why Greenpeace and other groups take this approach—it's the nature of advocacy. The end of saving the environment justifies the means of bending or breaking the truth. When environmental progress occurs—and it most certainly does—it can be, well, an inconvenient truth.

The American public itself has mixed attitudes about the condition of the environment. In a 2010 poll, 41% percent of Americans reported thinking that the environment is getting better, 48% said it is getting worse, and 11% thought it is staying about the same or they had no opinion.[10] Gallup polls have documented Americans' environmental attitudes by asking survey respondents if they personally worry about various environmental issues. As shown in Figure 9.1, currently Americans worry most about water, with almost half worrying a great deal about pollution in rivers and lakes. Below that, almost two-fifths of Americans worry a great deal about air pollution, and about one-third worry about the loss of the rain forest, the extinction of animal species, and global warming. Somewhat surprisingly, given the steady supply of environmental alarmism, Americans' worries about the environment are declining somewhat. The percentage of Americans worrying a great deal about water pollution, air pollution, the rain forest, and extinctions have dropped since the late 1980s. Only with global warming have worry levels remained stable. This lessened worry might reflect the overall

Figure 9.1: Do You Personally Worry About This Environmental Problem?

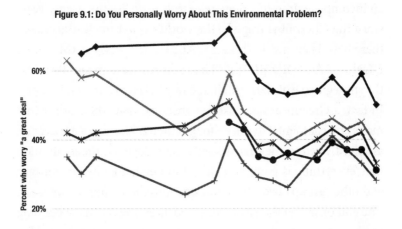

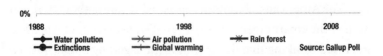

improving condition of the environment itself. Or it might result from increased worry about the economy, for these two concerns—the environment and the economy—are often inversely correlated.[11]

Before getting to data about the actual condition of the environment, I would like to introduce you to a fascinating figure in the environmental debate. Bjorn Lomborg is a statistician at the University of Aarhus in Denmark. Some view him as a modern-day Galileo—reinterpreting the physical world—while others cast him as disreputable and even evil. If nothing else, he's angered more environmentalists than perhaps anyone whose first name isn't President and last name isn't Bush. While I don't agree with Lomborg on every point, he has certainly influenced my thinking on environmental matters.

Here's his story. One day in 1997, Lomborg was in a Los Angeles bookstore browsing an issue of *Wired* magazine, in which he read an interview with controversial economist Julian Simon.[12] Simon argued that the doomsday view of the environment is incorrect, being based on preconceptions and poor statistics. This agitated Lomborg. Himself a left-wing member of Greenpeace, he viewed it as yet another example of American right-wing propaganda. So Lomborg set out to prove Simon wrong. There was just one problem: He couldn't. After years of study, Lomborg concluded that Simon was basically correct, and Lomborg wrote the bestselling book *The Skeptical Environmentalist*. (Along with changing his beliefs, Lomborg has changed his persona. Judging from his early book covers, he was a genial if perhaps slightly nerdy academic. Now, however, he's a celebrity. He made *Esquire*'s list of most influential people, and he has an edgier, cooler "look." Who knows, if my book sells well, I might get a new shirt or change my $15 haircut.)

Lomborg's approach appeals to me because he tries to go wherever the data takes him, even if it's against his initial assumptions. In contrast, too many researchers seem to find whatever it is they expected to find in the first place—using data to illustrate their preconceptions rather than systematically basing their conclusions on data.

Lomborg's data-first approach to the environment has gotten him into trouble. Apparently there's something called the Danish Committee on Scientific Dishonesty, and it ruled that Lomborg's book was not "scientifically honest," i.e., that it was contrary to the standards of good science. Ouch. Ultimately, the Danish Ministry of Science, Technology and Innovation overruled the Dishonesty Committee, noting that their ruling was not backed by documentation or argumentation. Nonetheless, this reaction to Lomborg's work, which is scrupulously documented, illustrates a more general view among some environmentalists: Criticism, no matter how well supported by the data, is akin to treason and should be ignored if not silenced.[13] The belief in environmental problems is akin to faith, and anyone who contradicts it must have an ulterior motive.[14]

Air Pollution

Let's take a look at the condition of several environmental problems starting with air pollution. It's no surprise that air pollution is really unhealthy. Smog contains a variety of problem-causing chemicals.[15] Nitrous oxides irritate lungs and cause respiratory infections. Carbon monoxide leads to visual and mental impairment and a decrease in manual dexterity. Fine particles get deep into lungs, causing asthma, bronchitis, and chronic coughing. Lead, even in small amounts, harms unborn children, bringing about miscarriages, retardation, paralysis, and low IQ. Ozone near the earth's surface decreases lung function.

The past several decades have witnessed some remarkably pessimistic rhetoric about air pollution. In 1970, *Life* magazine promised its readers that within a decade, urban dwellers would have to wear gas masks to survive air pollution, and only half as much sunlight would reach earth.[16] John Kenneth Galbraith wrote that when the

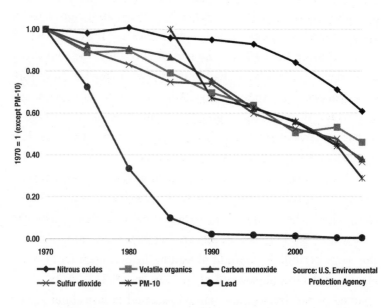

Figure 9.2: Air Pollution Emissions, 1970-2008

Source: U.S. Environmental Protection Agency

penultimate Western man is stalled in a traffic jam, succumbing to carbon monoxide, he would regret the focus on economic growth at any cost.[17] Even as recently as 2001, the Sierra Club claimed that "smog is out of control in almost all of our major cities."[18]

In reality, American air quality is getting better. Figure 9.2 plots emission levels since 1970 for six common air contaminants: nitrous oxides, volatile organics, carbon monoxide, sulfur dioxide, fine particles (10 microns wide or less), and lead. To facilitate comparison, I set the 1970 levels of each of these pollutants at 1 and then tracked how they changed over time relative to their 1970 level. As shown, all six pollutants have dropped substantially. Relative to 1970, the United States currently emits only 60% as much nitrous oxides, less than half the volatile organic compounds, and about a third of the carbon monoxide, sulfur dioxide, and fine particles. Lead emission is down to .5% (not a typo) of its 1970 levels.

America's improved air quality is reflected in the Environmental

Protection Agency's Air Quality Index. This index measures air pollution. The lower the score, the better; anything above 100 is considered a bad air day. In 1990, Los Angeles had 182 days in which it scored more than 100 on the Air Quality Index—about every other day—but by 2008 it had only 53 days. Likewise, New York City dropped from 56 to 29 days, Atlanta from 67 to 24 days, and so on. Overall, ten of the largest American cities had an average of 53 bad air days in 1990, and this dropped to an average of 19 days in 2008—a 63% drop in just eighteen years.

To appreciate just how much better things have gotten, consider a couple of success stories. In 1978, over 200,000 tons of lead were released into the air in the United States, but by 1998 this dropped to less than 4,000 tons—an astounding 98% reduction.[19] During this same period, the amount of lead in the average infant's blood also dropped to one-seventh of its 1970 level.[20] This drop, which resulted in part from cleaner air, is estimated to save about 22,000 lives a year.[21]

Another success story involves the ozone layer. In the mid-1980s, scientists figured out that the ozone layer was thinning due to humans' use of chlorofluorocarbons—which were popularly used in spray cans, refrigerators, and air-conditioners. The increased UV rays resulted in more skin cancer, premature aging of the skin, and eye diseases. In response to this threat, the production and use of chlorofluorocarbons were severely restricted, and as a result the ozone layer is slowly recovering.[22]

The drop in air pollution is all the more remarkable when we juxtapose it with society's growth over the past forty years. From 1970 to 2008, the United States' gross domestic product increased by 200%, Americans drove 160% more miles, and both energy consumption and population size grew by almost 50%.[23] This type of growth produces pollution, so if the United States' energy policies and practices had remained at 1970 levels, we would have seen a marked increase in pollution levels. Instead, pollution dropped substantially, even during this time of growth.

The drop in air pollution is due mainly to governmental regulation. In 1967, the U.S. government set exhaust requirements for cars, and it has regularly tightened them since. The government also created the Environmental Protection Agency, charged with setting standards for air quality. Clean Air Acts bolster both research into air pollution and control of it. In the end, the hot air in Washington has made clean skies for the rest of us.

Actually, in some parts of the world, air quality has been improving for a long time. One study has estimated the amount of air pollution in London going back to the year 1585 (based on population density and the amount of coal burned).[24] The amount of smoke and sulfur in London's air rose steadily from 1585 to the early 1700s, at which point it leveled off for about a century. Then, in the 1800s, with the industrial revolution, the amount of both sulfur and smoke in London skies shot up dramatically, reaching its peak in the 1890s. Over the last century, however, the amount of smoke and sulfur has steadily declined such that the London air now is as clean as it was before the mid-1700s.

Compared to the rest of the world, the United States has fairly clean air. In a ranking of the world's largest cities, Cairo and Delhi have the dirtiest air, with more than 150 micrograms of fine particles (PM-10) per cubic meter. A number of cities in China are next on the list. The worst American city is Los Angeles, ranked at 64, with 32 micrograms of fine particles in the air. While this is still a lot, it's only one-fifth of Cairo and Delhi and about one-third of Beijing.[25]

Water Pollution

Regarding water quality, in the early 1970s the U.S. government started a program to measure water quality in rivers, streams, and lakes throughout the country. The program measures biological data (e.g., how much life is supported), chemical data, (e.g., pesticides and toxins), physical data (e.g., temperature and pH levels), and microbiological data (such as bacteria from sewage). In 1972, only 30% to 40% of the wild water in the United States was deemed safe for fishing, swimming, or as a source of drinking water. Today, however, 60% to 70% of waters meet water-quality goals.[26]

This rise in water quality can be appreciated with a specific case study. An iconic moment in the modern environmental movement happened when the Cuyahoga River in Cleveland caught fire in June 1969. Now, I'm not a hydrologist, but I'm pretty sure water isn't supposed to do that. While the fire itself burned for only twenty minutes, it sparked ridicule of Cleveland and national concern about water quality. In the 1980s, when the EPA assessed the fish population on the stretch of river between Akron and Cleveland, they would sometimes come back with counts of ten. Not ten species of fish, but ten actual fish. Even lower forms of aquatic life, such as leeches and sludge worms, which will live almost anywhere, refused to live in the Cuyahoga. Fast-forward to the present and it's an entirely different story. Recent monitoring of the Cuyahoga has found forty different species of fish, including steelhead trout and northern pike. Soon the river is expected to meet the government's stringent standard for being a healthy environment for aquatic life.

In regards to safe drinking water, nearly all Americans have it. As early as 1870, American cities used sand filtration to clean their water; chlorination was introduced in 1908.[27] We have drunk clean water for so long that we take it for granted, but imagine what life would be like without it. Typhoid is a water-borne bacterial disease that's been virtually eliminated in the United States. However, if we had typhoid rates today as high as they were in 1900, around 80,000 Americans would die from it each year—five times more than died of AIDS at its peak.[28] Instead, fewer than a dozen Americans die each year due to faulty water systems.[29]

Worldwide, a useful distinction is made between improved and unimproved drinking water. (Hint: you want the improved water.)[30] Improved water is from a protected well, spring, or municipal source. Unimproved water, in contrast, comes from unprotected wells or springs. Figure 9.3 shows worldwide access to improved water.[31] In 1990, 77% of the world's population had improved water, and now it's up to 87%. Developed regions, such as the United States, have had nearly 100% improved water for some time now, so the gains were made mostly in the developing regions of the world. East Asia went from 69% improved water to 89%, Southeast Asia from 72% to 86%, and Sub-Saharan Africa from 49% to 60%. Only Oceania remained level at about 50%. Even with all these gains, however, an estimated 1.1 billion people—approximately four times the population of the United States—do not have access to safe water.[32]

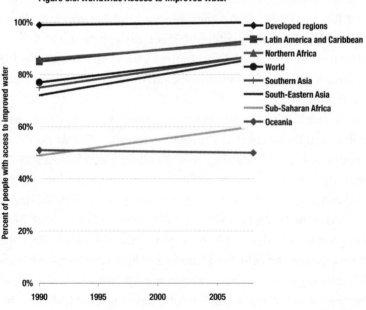

Figure 9.3: Worldwide Access to Improved Water

Source: United Nations

189

Christians Making a Difference

In 1990, a group of Christians from Houston, Texas, traveled to Kenya, where they saw the desperate need for clean drinking water. Upon their return, they founded Living Water International, an organization that equips local people to drill wells, repair pumps, and practice safe hygiene. Most of Living Water's projects involve drilling new wells or rehabilitating old ones, but they also create protected springs and rainwater catchment systems. Any given water project can provide water for hundreds to thousands of people, depending on the water aquifer and the surrounding population. To date, Living Water has completed over nine thousand water projects in twenty-five different countries.[33]

Deforestation

Working my way through the four basic elements, it's time for earth. (I don't think I'll get to fire.) A critical aspect of land use is the amount of earth covered by forests. Forests serve vital functions. They ameliorate global warming by absorbing carbon dioxide, and they support biodiversity because some plants and animals just like the forest. Sometimes, however, forests are cleared and the land is converted to other uses, such as agriculture and infrastructure. This is called deforestation. Conversely, sometimes the reverse happens, with agricultural and other land being returned to forest land.[34]

Before Europeans settled in the United States, an estimated 1 billion acres were covered with mature forests.[35] This works out to about one-half of the land mass of the modern-day United States.[36] Starting with the colonists, settlers cleared forests for agricultural and urban use. Deforestation accelerated in the late 1800s, and it peaked in the 1920s, by which time about 750 million acres of forest land remained—down 25% from pre-settlement times. Since the 1920s, the amount of forested land in the United States has remained fairly steady due to countering pressures. America loses forest land because of urban sprawl, agriculture, reservoirs, natural disasters, and fires. However, it gains forest land through fire suppression, marginal farmland returning to forest (especially in the East), and large-scale plantings of forests (especially in the South).[37]

The process of reforestation is abundant here in Connecticut, where I live. In the 1800s, only about 35% of the state was covered by forest, but now it's up to around 60%.[38] The land has lots and lots of rocks in it, so it wasn't suitable farmland when farming became mechanized at the start of the twentieth century. Combines and other farm machines don't like rocky, hilly terrain, so farms were abandoned and returned to their natural, forested state. As a result, when you go for a hike, no matter how deep in the woods you go, you see rock walls, house foundations, and old wagon trails—remnants of an earlier time.

Worldwide, deforestation is a bigger problem, though there is room for optimism. Currently about one-third of the earth's land is covered with forest, but this is down 20% from historical times.[39] As shown in Figure 9.4, the loss of forestland has varied widely by continent.[40] From 1990 to 2000, the worldwide loss of forestland was .22% a year, resulting in a total loss of 2.2% over the decade. Since 2000, the annual loss rate has dropped to 1.8%. South America and Africa have lost the most forestland. In recent years, the annual loss rate on these continents was .5%. Brazil and Indonesia were the individual countries that lost the most forestland. As of 2005, Brazil lost .6% of its forestland each year, which may not seem like much, but the Amazon forest is so big that this constitutes a whopping 42% of global forest loss that year. In 2005, Indonesia was losing a remarkable 2% of its forestland each year—25% of the total world loss. On the positive side, both countries are slowing down their deforestation.[41]

Worldwide, deforestation occurs because many forests, especially those in the tropics, have either no property rights or poorly administered rights.[42] This situation results in what economists term "the tragedy of the commons"—many people have an incentive to

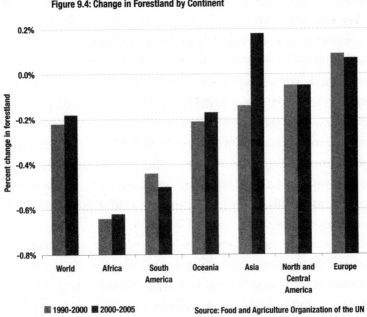

Figure 9.4: Change in Forestland by Continent

■ 1990-2000 ■ 2000-2005   Source: Food and Agriculture Organization of the UN

log the forests, but few have a direct incentive to maintain them. Farmers will clear a forested area and farm it for a few years until the soil is depleted, and then clear another area. National governments generate substantial cash by selling forestland to multinational companies. Also, it's estimated that between one-quarter to one-half of people in developing countries use firewood for fuel. This is especially true in Africa, where many cities have little to no available firewood within twenty miles. These pressures lead to greater forest loss in the poorest nations.[43]

Some countries, however, are actually gaining forestland. Sometimes forests experience natural growth—expanding their existing boundaries. Even more so, they expand with replanting. Currently about 7% of all forestland worldwide is planted forest.[44] China, in particular, has converted substantial portions of land into forests, offsetting losses in forest area elsewhere in the world. In fact, without

China's extensive replanting, global forest loss would be 80% greater than it is. China replants more forest area each year than Brazil loses.[45] India, Vietnam, and Spain have also replanted considerable forest area.

Deforestation would be much, much worse if it were not for advances in agriculture. As discussed previously, agricultural productivity is at an all-time high; this means that farmers can get more crops out of the same amount of land. This in turn lessens the pressure to convert forests into farmland. Economist Indur Goklany estimates that if agricultural yields were still at 1961 levels, the world would need to convert to farmland an additional area the size of South America (without Chile) just to feed itself.[46]

An ironic story illustrates the difficulties of preserving the world's forests in the face of profit incentives. Children's books often trumpet the need to save the rain forests. This ecological message appeals to children, and it lends itself to illustration, with exotic trees and brightly colored animals. A rain forest activist group examined these save-the-rain-forest books more carefully, and it turns out that 60% of them were printed on paper from Indonesia's threatened rain forests.[47]

Global Warming

Now for a topic that I've worried about addressing since I began writing this book: global warming. Not only is the science complex

---

Christians Making a Difference

Target Earth, based in Tempe, Arizona, is an organization with the mission of serving the earth and serving the poor. Out of devotion for God, they work toward a sustainable future. Among their projects is the Eden Conservancy. This program raises money to buy and protect the world's endangered lands. One such purchase was of Jaguar Creek—eight thousand acres of rain forest in Belize, Central America. Not only does this purchase stave off deforestation, but it also provides a refuge for animals. Target Earth has created a Christian-based environmental stewardship program centered on Jaguar Creek.[48]

(and I'm just a simple sociologist), but it's a highly politicized topic, making it easy to unintentionally offend people. Furthermore, much of the discussion on this issue regards what will happen in the future rather than what has already happened, and the future is so difficult to know accurately. Nonetheless, here goes.

When scientists measure the temperature of the earth's surface, they don't focus on its average temperature worldwide, because this would require a comprehensive sample of places around the world. Instead, scientists measure *temperature anomalies*—estimates of how temperatures have changed relative to the past. It's a reasonably well-accepted fact that both land and sea have heated up over the past century. Figure 9.5 presents estimates compiled by the National OAA on the global surface temperature anomalies for both land and sea since 1880. The baseline (or 0 point) is the average temperature during the twentieth century. As shown, global surface temperatures steadily rose from about 1900 to 1940. From 1940 to 1980, they dropped a bit and rebounded, and from the 1980s they have risen at a fairly rapid rate. As a result of these changes, the world is about 2° Fahrenheit warmer than it was in the 1880s.

This global warming is probably the cause of lots of changes in the world.[49] According to the Environmental Protection Agency, the sea level is rising about an inch a decade, there is less ice in the Arctic, and glaciers worldwide are diminishing. Lakes in northern regions are staying frozen for less time during winter. Growing seasons are starting earlier, plants are blooming earlier, and birds are spending their winters farther north.

However, it's my impression that the greatest concern about global warming is not what has happened so far but what might happen in the future. Politicians and activists have filled the future with dire predictions. U.N. Secretary General Ban-Ki-Moon has declared climate change "the defining challenge of our age."[50] Climate-control advocates predict that global warming will create

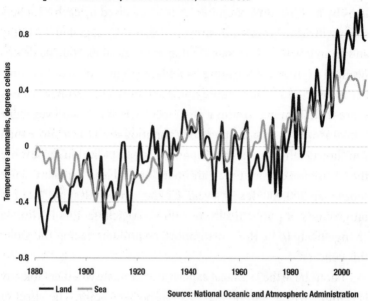

Figure 9.5: Global Temperature Anomalies, Land and Sea

Source: National Oceanic and Atmospheric Administration

mass economic and political instability, as refugees flee areas buffeted by floods, droughts, famine, and rising seas.[51] The Worldwatch Institute describes an apocalypse:

> It is now virtually certain that children born today will find their lives preoccupied by an inexorably warming world. Food supplies will be diminished, and many of the world's forests will be destroyed. Not just the coral reefs that nurture many fisheries, but the chemistry of the oceans will face disruption. Indeed the world's oceans are already acidifying rapidly. Coastlines will be rearranged, and so will the world's wetlands. Whether you are a farmer or an office worker, whether you live in the northern or southern hemisphere, whether you are rich or poor, you will be affected.[52]

A more moderate view of global warming analyzes its impact relative to other world problems. Indur Goklany, a scientist with the Office of Policy Analysis for the U.S. Department of the Interior, has compared the estimated impact of global warming versus other problems by looking at the number of deaths caused by each. Goklany starts with a fairly extreme estimate of the effect of global warming, and from this he extrapolates that in the year 2000, 160,000 deaths resulted from global warming.[53] Goklany points out that this number is dwarfed by other, more mundane problems. Hunger causes more than 3 million deaths a year; insufficient fruit and vegetable intake as well as unsafe water and sanitation each cause more than 2 million deaths a year; malaria and indoor air pollution cause more than 1 million deaths; urban air pollution and lead exposure cause more than 200,000 deaths a year. Goklany concludes that "neither on grounds of public health nor on ecological factors is climate change likely to be the most important problem facing the globe this century."[54]

I don't have the technical expertise to evaluate whether Goklany is right or wrong, but he makes an important point. The effect of global warming must be examined in light of other problems. Just because global warming is harmful—and it certainly appears so—doesn't necessarily mean that it automatically takes first place in the world-problem sweepstakes. This raises a broader issue, one that I will elaborate on in the next chapter, that the response to any problem should be proportional to the harm it causes. Furthermore, radical solutions to global warming, such as an extreme cutback in the use of fossil fuel, could potentially cause more harm than good.[55] For example, fossil fuels make it possible to feed many people inexpensively, and to unduly limit them could increase human suffering. I don't know the optimal balance, but I think that finding it is the key.

What will happen in the future with global warming? It's difficult to know with any accuracy because predictions rely on numerous assumptions about weather, atmosphere, economic growth, fossil fuel use, and the size of the world's population. If these assumptions are wrong, so too are the corresponding predictions. World temperatures have steadily risen over the last thirty years, but that doesn't mean they will continue to do so. As shown in Figure 9.5, global temperatures have sometimes declined and sometimes stayed the same. To illustrate how quickly temperature trends can reverse, *Time* magazine in the 1970s actually warned of a coming ice age.[56] Still, global warming is something to be concerned about.

Wealth and the Environment

Economic activity is often blamed for environmental problems. Either we're taking too many resources out of the environment, as with deforestation, or we're putting too much waste into it, as with air pollution. Al Gore, in his book *Earth in the Balance*, illustrates this perspective as he writes that we have been mortgaging our environmental future through our mindless pursuit of economic growth.[57]

It turns out, however, that richer countries actually take better care of the environment than do poorer countries. We can see this using the Environmental Protection Index, created by scientists at Yale and Columbia Universities. It ranks countries on twenty-five measures of environmental health and ecosystem vitality, including forestry and forest cover, fisheries, agriculture, pesticide regulation, greenhouse emissions, air pollution, water quality and scarcity, biodiversity and habitat, and marine protection (the ocean, not soldiers). A high score on this index reflects a country doing well in taking care of its natural environment.

The countries with the highest Index scores are Iceland (94 out of 100), Switzerland (89), Costa Rica (86), and Sweden (86). The lowest-scoring countries are Sierra Leone (32), Central African Republic (33), Mauritania (33), Angola (36), and Togo (36). Obviously the highest-scoring countries are much wealthier than the lowest-scoring countries. To illustrate the relationship between wealth and environmental protection, I grouped nations of the world (from which Environmental Protection Index data is available) into eight groups by their average gross domestic product per capita. These groups were countries with per-capita GDPs of less than $1,000 a year (40 countries); $1,000 to $2,000 (20 countries); $2,000 to $4,000 (23 countries); $4,000 to $7,000 (19 countries); $7,000 to $15,000 (17 countries); $15,000 to $30,000 (20 countries); $30,000 to $45,000 (13 countries); and more than $45,000 (11 countries). I then calculated the average Environmental Protection Index score for each of the eight groups, and I plotted the result in Figure 9.6. As you can see, there is an overall positive relationship between wealth and environmental stewardship.[58] The countries with per-capita incomes of $45,000 or more scored an average of 74.5, compared to 65 for countries with per-capita incomes in the $7,000 to $15,000 range, and 47 for countries with a per-capita income of less than $1,000 a year.

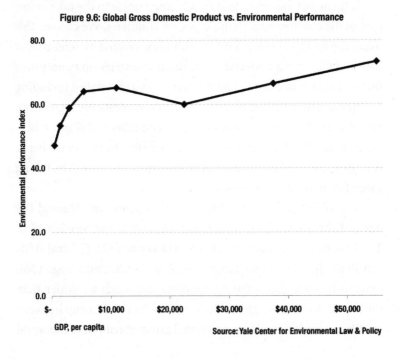

Figure 9.6: Global Gross Domestic Product vs. Environmental Performance

Source: Yale Center for Environmental Law & Policy

Where does the United States rank on the Environmental Protection Index? We score 63.5—number 60 out of 163, and tied with Paraguay. Estonia, Sri Lanka, and Georgia are just above us; Brazil, Poland, and Venezuela just behind us. Yale Professor Daniel Esty, chief author of the Environmental Performance Index, makes an interesting observation about the United States' ranking. He has found that Americans wonder why we're so low, since we like to be the best at everything, while Europeans wonder how the United States scores so high, since they see us as an environmental hazard.[59]

Wealthier countries take better care of the environment because they have the resources with which to do so. In contrast, poorer countries have to focus on more immediate issues of human survival, and environmental protection can be a luxury. Furthermore, efforts to protect the environment in poorer countries can run afoul of corrupt governments, inefficient bureaucracy, unenforced property rights, and inadequate legal systems.[60] This raises an interesting possibility—that economic growth is the key to a cleaner world.[61] It could well be that the most effective way of improving the environment worldwide is to help poorer countries develop their economies.

CHAPTER 10

THE COUNTING
OF BLESSINGS

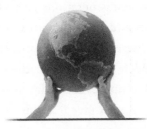

Someone said to Voltaire "Life is hard." He replied? "Compared to what?"
—*Referenced by Julian Simon, economist*[1]

People living in the middle class in the U.S. live better than 99.4% of all human beings who have ever existed.
—*Greg Easterbrook, writer*[2]

I decline to accept the end of man. . . . I believe that man will not merely endure; he will prevail.
—*William Faulkner*[3]

Congratulations. You've made it to the end of the book, and I will try to reward you with a conclusion that is both interesting and informative. Initially, I asked my editor if I could perform an interpretive dance and post a video of it online, but he encouraged me to stay with the more traditional writing. So I will summarize my findings and then give some explanations for why the world is getting better in so many ways. I finish with some thoughts about what you, the reader, can do in response to the material covered in this book. (Your own interpretive dance perhaps?)

An Overview of Findings

As a way to summarize the findings of this book all in one place, I've created a table. This table takes the issues covered in this book and codes them by whether things have gotten better, worse, or stayed the same since 1950 and since 1980. (I picked thirty-year intervals to represent generations.) This table has three columns. The first column identifies an area of life, such as family income. Unless otherwise specified, these columns refer to life in the United States (which I focus on because of data limitations). The second column compares life today versus 1980. If life has gotten substantially better, I give it a plus or two depending on how much so. If it has stayed the same, I give it a zero. If it's gotten worse, I give it a minus or two. The third column does the same comparing today to 1950. This table provides a simple visual representation of how things have changed—pluses are good, minuses are bad.

Figure 10.1:
Life in the United States Today
Compared to 30 and 60 Years Ago.

Topic Measure	Life Today Compared to:	
	1980	1950
Economics		
Family income	+	++
Poverty rate	o	++
Income inequality	-	--
Unemployment	-	--
Cost of living	+	++

| Topic | Life Today Compared to: | |
Measure	1980	1950
Savings	-	-
Debt	-	-
Smarts		
Education	+	++
Literacy	o	+
Intelligence	+	++
Health		
Life expectancy	+	++
Infant mortality	++	++
Infectious diseases	o	++
Cancer	o	+
HIV	o	--
Cigarette smoking	++	++
Obesity	--	--
World hunger	+	++
Accidents	+	++
Sense of Well-Being		
Happiness	o	o
Suicide	+	+
Television watching	-	--
Leisure time	+	+
War and Freedom		
Crime	++	o
Prisoners	--	--
Global Wars	++	++
Prejudice	+	++
Global freedom	++	++
Relationships		
Living together	--	--
Divorce	+	--

	Life Today Compared to:	
Topic		
Measure	**1980**	**1950**
Single-parent families	-	--
Family life	o	o
Sexual behavior	o	--
Sexual attitudes	o	-
Abortions	+	--
Environment		
Air quality	++	+
Water quality	+	
Forests	o	o
Global warming	-	--

++ Substantially better
+ Somewhat better
o About the same
- Somewhat worse
-- Substantially worse

Before jumping into the details of the table, let me point out some of its limitations. It's a simplification, and as with all simplifications, it leaves out many nuances and qualifications. Also, not every area of life summarized is of equal importance. And even if an area of life is getting better, it might not be getting better fast enough to suit some people. Finally, the table is limited to changes in the past sixty years, but as discussed in this book, some changes have been unfolding over centuries and even millennia.

With these caveats in mind, have things gotten better? In several areas of life there is a lot of good news. As shown in Figure 10.1, we Americans are much healthier now than before. We live much longer, and this is arguably the single most important indicator in the whole table. Fewer children die, we have fewer diseases and accidents, and there's less hunger in the world. On the downside, though, we Americans are getting rather chubby.

We are better educated, more literate, and perhaps overall

smarter than in the past. We have less crime. Worldwide, fewer people die in wars, and more people live under democracy. Unfortunately, though, the United States incarcerates a remarkably high percentage of its citizens.

In other areas of life the news is still positive but more mixed. Economically, family income is up and the cost of living is down. Unemployment is cyclical (though we're in the midst of high unemployment now), and, unfortunately, income inequality is on the rise. Also, Americans have too much debt and too little savings. With general well-being, Americans have more leisure time, there are fewer suicides, and our self-reported happiness is mostly stable. On the downside, we're absolutely glued to our televisions. Are we really happy if we watch so many reality TV shows?

When it comes to the environment, air and water quality has improved and deforestation is slowing down. But the earth is warming up—and that may be a real problem in the future.

The one area with a preponderance of bad news is social relationships. Relative to 1950, marriage and two-parent families are less frequent, and cohabitation, divorce, sexual promiscuity, and abortions are much more frequent. A bit of good news: In recent decades, divorce and abortion rates have slowly declined.

I started this book with the simple question of whether life is getting better, and my answer is "mostly yes." Think of it this way: Is there any other period in history when people were better off than now? I don't see one. Some people hold the 1950s as the good ol' days, but going back to the '50s would entail having less money, higher expenses, inferior health care, less education, and shorter lives. Women would have far fewer job opportunities and many blacks wouldn't be able to vote. Worldwide, there would be far more war and starvation. Would you really want that?

What about living the simple life as a peasant long ago? Well, you'd better hope you didn't get sick and need quality health care. Also, get ready for long hours of work for relatively sparse food. If your crop is hit with disease or drought, you might be instantly destitute.[4]

While this book has focused on how life has changed over time, in various places it also examines the quality of life across places, and here I would like to identify those places that are doing the best. Starting with the United States, the Institute for Innovation of Social Policy ranks the social health of all fifty states.[5] For each state it measures sixteen different indicators including infant mortality, child and elderly poverty, teen and elderly suicide, teen drug abuse, education, unemployment, average wages, health insurance coverage, homicides, drunk-driving fatalities, affordable housing, and income inequality. Put together, the sixteen measures constitute the Social Health Index, which ranges from 1 to 100. Figure 10.2 presents the social health scores for each of the fifty states divided into four groups. The states that have very good social health include Minnesota, Iowa, and New Hampshire; good states include Wisconsin, Maryland, and South Dakota; fair states include New York, Georgia, and Nevada; and poor states include Arkansas, Kentucky, and Tennessee.

Several patterns emerge in this ranking. For the most part, northern states do better than southern states. Of the thirteen states that share a border with Canada (I had to look it up on a map—I forgot Idaho), ten rate as either very good or good. In marked contrast, seven of the states on the southern border rate as poor, and one, California, rates fair. The highest-scoring states tend to be in the Northeast or the Midwest, and the lowest are in the South and West. Race and ethnicity also matters. The states that rate very good or good have a median of 84.7% and 81.7% whites, whereas the fair states have a median of 70.8% and poor states 65.1%. This is further testimony to the racial inequality that exists in our country.

Figure 10.2: The Social Health of States

Social Health	States (Scores)	Median Percent White
Very good (Score 60 or above)	Minnesota (75), Iowa (71), New Hampshire (67), Nebraska (67), Hawaii (63), Vermont (63), Connecticut (61), North Dakota (61), Utah (61), New Jersey (60), Idaho (60), Virginia (60)	84.7%
Good (Score 50-59)	Pennsylvania (59), Maine (57), Indiana (56), Kansas (56), Delaware (56), Illinois (55), Wisconsin (55), Maryland (55), South Dakota (54), Ohio (54), Wyoming (53), Massachusetts (53), Washington (52), Missouri (51)	81.7%
Fair (Score 40-49)	Michigan (49), Oregon (48), Rhode Island (47), Colorado (45), New York (44), Georgia (44), Alaska (44), Nevada (43), California (42), West Virginia (41), Oklahoma (40)	70.8%
Poor (Score 39 or below)	Montana (39), Alabama (39), South Carolina (38), Texas (38), Louisiana (38), Arkansas (36), Kentucky (36), Tennessee (36), Florida (34), North Carolina (33), Arizona (33), Mississippi (31), New Mexico (27)	65.1%

Worldwide, the United Nations produces a similar index of well-being for countries—the Human Development Index. It is based on three measures: life expectancy, education, and income. Figure 10.3 is a map of the world that codes countries by how they score on the Human Development Index. The regions scoring highest include Central and Northern Europe, the United States, Canada, and Australia. Below them, but still above average, are Russia, Eastern Europe, Brazil, and several other South American countries. In the middle of the pack are most of the countries between Turkey and China, as well as countries in northeast South America. At the bottom of the ratings are most of the countries in Africa.

The United Nations has calculated this index for several decades now, so we can see how many countries are better off over time. The United Nations has collected data on 115 countries from 1990 to 2007, and would you like to guess how many of them had improved

Figure 10.3

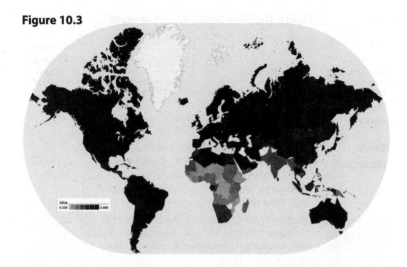

over this time period? If you guessed 109, you are absolutely right. The biggest gainers included Mali, Mozambique, Rwanda, Uganda, Bangladesh, and Burkino Faso—countries that really needed it. Only six countries got worse—Zambia, Swaziland, South Africa, Tajikistan, Moldova, and Russia.

Why Are So Many Things Getting Better?

When people explain why the world is getting better, they often point to a particular invention or development such as antibiotics or improved agricultural practices. The economist Julian Simon, however, has identified a broader process at work. According to Simon, serious problems regularly arise in the world that, left unchecked, would cause significant harm.[6] However—and this is Simon's main point—problems are not left unchecked. Instead, human effort and ingenuity solves or ameliorates most, if not all, problems. From Simon's perspective, society has short-term problems but long-term solutions. As he puts it, "Almost every economic and social change or trend points in the positive direction, as long as we view the matter over a reasonably long period of time. That is, all aspects of material human welfare are improving in the aggregate."[7] Here's the really cool part. As good as things are now, if Simon is right, then life will keep getting better.

Simon's perspective also helps us to understand why people are so pessimistic about the present—it's a problem of extrapolation. In the short term, some aspects of society do get worse, and the root of fear and pessimism is projecting today's downturns into the future.[8] As an example of this type of extrapolation, someone in the nineteenth century predicted that the number of horses needed to serve London by the year 1950 would cover its streets with ten feet of manure.[9] Thankfully, this hasn't happened in London. There's no guarantee that humans will solve all of our problems in the long run, but we have a pretty good track record. The problem with which we've had the most trouble seems to be pessimism—we believe that life is getting worse no matter how much it improves.[10]

Why have humans gotten so good at solving problems in recent centuries? After all, many infectious diseases abounded for millennia before being cured in the last hundred years or so. Science writer Matt Ridley offers a compelling explanation by pointing to two underlying processes—specialization and exchange. As workers and companies specialize, they create products much better and much cheaper than could be done otherwise. As a result, more good things are available to more people. Ridley describes an experiment that illustrates the power of specialization.[11] A researcher at Drexel University set out to make a men's suit using only materials produced within one hundred miles of her home. Ultimately, this suit required five hundred hours of work by twenty different artisans, and cost about a hundred times that of a similar suit bought at a department store. In a similar vein, an artist decided to make a toaster from scratch. It took him many months and lots of money to make a toaster inferior to what you can buy cheaply at the store.

Specialization by itself doesn't work without exchange. What good is making thousands of toasters inexpensively if you only sell to your neighbors? ("Hey, Fred, you look like you need some more toast.") If instead you can sell your toasters throughout the country or world, then you can sell plenty and have the money to buy products made elsewhere. Worldwide exchange allows us to buy the best products for the cheapest prices, and the world's transportation system—planes, ships, trains, and trucks—make this exchange possible. To appreciate the magnitude of this exchange, walk down any aisle of your grocery store. The other day I bought produce raised in California, Florida, Texas, Mexico, Chile, and Israel. You can also look at the labels on your clothes. Right now I'm wearing a shirt made in Nicaragua, a Polartec jacket from China, pants from Mexico, and L.L. Bean, moosehide slippers from Canada. I don't have to fly to Central America to buy shirts (though I actually did once—but that's another story). Instead, they are shipped to the United States and end up in the store down the road.

Even more important than exchanging things is exchanging information, which has gone into hyperdrive with the Internet. The data presented in this book was collected worldwide at the cost of many millions of dollars. I accessed it in my office for free or at minimal cost from academic journals, data repositories, or online sites. This ready exchange of information allows people to become experts in different areas. Two months ago, back when I was writing chapter 8, I had my gall bladder removed. The surgeon used laparoscopic surgery, which necessitated only four small incisions in my abdomen. Now, my surgeon is a smart guy, but he didn't invent this method himself. Instead, he learned it from others. What if this surgical information had never been exchanged? Back in the day, doctors removed gall bladders using a big, long incision across the abdomen, and it left quite a scar. If you want to know why I appreciate the exchange of surgical information, search the Internet for a picture of Lyndon Johnson showing reporters his gall bladder surgery scar. Not a pretty sight. In sum, long-term problem solving, via specialization and exchange, has made our world a much better place to live.

What is the most important invention in history? Obviously this subjective question elicits a variety of answers. Julian Simon himself identified electricity, drugs, and the microchip.[12] Other scholars highlight the importance of agricultural technology.[13] My favorite answer to this question, however, comes from a survey of four thousand British consumers. They were asked to identify the greatest inventions of history, and at number one they put the wheel. It was followed by the airplane (2), light bulb (3), Internet (4), personal computers (5), telephone (6), penicillin (8), flushing toilet (9), combustion engine (10), contraceptive pill (11), washing machine (12), central heating (13), refrigerator (14), painkillers (15), steam engine (15), freezer (17), camera (18), cars (19), eyeglasses (20), and sociology (21). (Okay, I made up that last one.) Now, if you're paying attention, you'll notice that I skipped number 7. It was the iPhone. That's right—British people think the iPhone is more important than penicillin, the internal combustion engine, and the toilet. Perhaps the iPhone has some great new apps that I don't know about.

Incentives to Help Others

While technology has advanced considerably, that doesn't fully answer why the world is getting better. After all, technological developments need not be aimed at helping other people. They could simply provide more luxury items instead of feeding the poor or healing the sick. Here is where motivation comes in. Thankfully, there is substantial motivation for people, companies, and governments to alleviate suffering and increase well-being. One source of motivation comes from financial and social incentives. A company that can solve people's problems is a company that will probably make lots of money. Consider the drug Lipitor. It lowers cholesterol, thus lowering the risk of heart attacks and strokes. Its development makes the world a better place. It is also the best-selling pharmaceutical drug in the world, with annual sales of almost 13 billion dollars for the drug company Pfizer.[14] Likewise, companies have made a lot of money by helping farmers grow more food or making housework easier or by providing any of a number of things that have helped make the world better.

But even when pro-social incentives do not exist in the marketplace, they can be created. An example of a created incentive is the X Prizes. This is a nonprofit, educational organization with the goal to "create radical breakthroughs for the benefit of humanity."[15] The X Prize Foundation has created competitions to design new technologies to benefit humanity, and it offers substantial cash prizes to the winners. For example, a current X Prize offers 1 million dollars to whoever can create a better way of cleaning oil spills in the ocean. There are future X Prizes planned for diagnosing tuberculosis, preserving biodiversity, and creating sustainable housing.

Altruism and Christian Love

Another reason that people do good is an internal motivation to help others—altruism. Even without financial or external incentives, countless people give unselfishly to others, and it's hard to overestimate how much good this does in the world. I'm not sure how one would measure the global impact of altruism because it is so pervasive and often hidden, and so it is perhaps best understood by illustration. This is why I have included stories throughout this book of people and organizations that are making the world a better place. Some altruism happens on a grand scale. For example, two of the world's richest people, Bill and Melinda Gates, have given billions of dollars to support health and development around the world. Their money has gone toward vaccinating children, finding a cure for AIDS and tuberculosis, eradicating malaria and polio, and supporting microfinance loans to the poorest of the poor. Other altruism happens on a much quieter, day-to-day basis. Listening to a friend's problems, helping a stranger in need, and volunteering for a good cause all make the world a better place.

I see this drive to altruism in my students. Some students just want whatever they can get out of life for themselves, and for them I'm happy to write law school recommendations. But other students make career plans with an eye toward making life better for others. I have had students go on to teach in poor neighborhoods, offer medical care to the needy, and counsel troubled youth.

People have varying opinions as to the origins of this altruistic impulse. Some believe it is a genetically encoded biological adaptation designed to promote the survival of our species. Others view it as socialization in the interests of creating a cohesive, functional group. As a Christian, I believe it is the human reflection of a loving God. Jesus Christ said that He did not come to be served but to serve, and we are called to emulate Him.

In my previous book, I examined the moral actions of Christians. As much as any group in American society, Christians demonstrate altruistic love. They spend time with friends and neighbors; they selflessly care for others; they give to charities; and they work with the downtrodden. While Christians are called to be altruistic, this trait is certainly not exclusive to Christians, for people of varying beliefs express it as well. This altruism, which is often fueled by Christian belief, makes the world a better place.

A Begrudging Nod Toward Activism

A last motivation for the world's continual improvement pains me to identify. You see, I'm not overly fond of some aspects of activism. As someone who works to present information accurately, I get frustrated with the exaggeration, misinformation, and

Christians Making a Difference

In 1998, six white kids fresh out of college wanted to live as Jesus did, so they bought a run-down house in inner-city Philadelphia and devoted themselves to loving God and loving others. They call themselves The Simple Way, and they number many more now. They want to give themselves over fully to the work of the community, so they work mostly part time so that they can give more attention to each other and the surrounding community. They created community gardens and shared meals with their neighbors. They started a flag-football league for local teens. They hang out with the local children and share life with their community. They pray together each morning with their friends and neighbors. They have family dinners on Friday nights. Basically, they put the relationships in their lives first, and they respond to the needs of others as they are able to. Their vision of Christianity is of a "community of people who have fallen desperately in love with God and with suffering people, and who allow those relationships to disturb and transform them."[16]

strategic hysteria offered by some activists, but I must admit that their strategies probably work to some extent. Recent decades have witnessed remarkable improvements in humans' quality of life, and this improvement has occurred in the context of strident advocacy. Quite likely, this advocacy has helped bring about some of the improvements. The clamor of advocates—whether they are environmentalists, naturalists, scientists, doctors, labor groups, lawyers, journalists, or writers—creates both the motivation and the opportunity to solve the problems they address.[17] As advocates define and promote problems, politicians, business leaders, scientists, and others step forward to solve them. To illustrate, the National Cancer Institute has an annual budget of around $5 billion; I imagine that their budget is so high in part due to the countless relays-for-life and walks-for-the-cure and different colored ribbons that have focused so much attention on cancer.[18]

Sociologist Amitai Etzioni describes the value of advocates as follows.[19] Elaborating on the boy-who-cried-wolf parable, Etzioni argues that healthy societies need those who will cry wolf at the merest shadow or rustling noise, as well as those who are more objective in their wolf-assessing skills. Taken together, the alarmist and the skeptic produce a balanced society in which problems are recognized but society is not overwhelmed with despair—a society that effectively deals with problems.

Having given a begrudging nod to alarmism, I think it could be scaled back considerably and still serve its purpose.

What Is Getting Worse?

In the midst of all this good news, we should not overlook that some aspects of life are indeed getting worse. Those covered in this book include income inequality, indebtedness, obesity, television watching, imprisonment rates, cohabitation, single-parent families, and global warming. Two themes emerge from these problems: overconsumption and disrupted social relationships. The most obvious example of overconsumption is obesity. There are far more overfed Americans than underfed Americans. We also consume copious amounts of fossil fuels, which contributes to global warming. We spend hours and hours a day watching television and other media. We borrow money to buy more things.

The disruption of social relationships is evidenced by changes in American family life. Cohabitation is rising, divorce rates are very high, and single-parent families are relatively common. Other studies have found evidence of increasing social autonomy and isolation in our society. Americans today, compared to twenty years ago, even have fewer people in whom they can confide.[20] Sociologist Robert Putnam notes that Americans now participate in fewer voluntary civic organizations and recreational groups than they used to, a phenomenon that he labels "bowling alone."[21]

What will happen in the future with these problems? An alarmist perspective would hold that they will get worse and worse, eventually causing incalculable suffering.

Another possibility is that these problems will fit Julian Simon's prediction of short-term problems and long-term solutions. Maybe these problems will diminish in the coming decades; in fact, society is working on most of them. For example, with global warming, there are countless initiatives to lessen carbon output.

Ironically, some of today's problems stem from yesterday's solutions. For example, the availability and low cost of food has reduced hunger, but it has also made obesity possible. Who wouldn't be overweight with Ben and Jerry's ice cream available everywhere? (Certainly not me.) Likewise, we have more money now, but this has led to social isolation. We can hire labor rather than trading it with others. We can buy equipment rather than borrowing it from our neighbors. In short, we don't "need" other people as much as we used to now that we can afford to be alone. I'm not advocating that we do away with readily available food, increased income, and other societal advances. Rather, I'm pointing out that solutions to problems often pose their own problems. As such, no matter how many problems are solved today, we will always have more in the future. This suggests a reconceptualization of Simon's axiom. Problem solving is not a linear process of identifying a problem and then solving it. Rather, it's an iterative process. Problems are identified, solutions are applied; solutions cause other problems, these other problems are identified and given solutions; problems arise from these secondary solutions, and so on. Social progress, then, comes not with the complete elimination of problems, but rather having tomorrow's problems be less severe and less costly than today's problems. We will always have problems; we just hope they will become smaller and smaller over time.

Another possibility regarding today's problems involves what we define as problems. Sometimes a problem goes away not because it actually gets better but because we stop considering it a problem. Now, it's hard to imagine this happening with some big problems.

Infant mortality, I imagine, will always be viewed as a problem. Other problems, however, are more ambiguous in nature. Americans used to define premarital sex as more of a problem than they do now, even though it continues at very high levels. We are starting to define a high imprisonment rate as more of a problem than we used to. Even with global warming there is divided opinion. Some view it as the greatest danger facing humankind, while others cast it off as a fabrication. The "social construction" (sociology lingo) of problems is a fascinating topic, albeit one outside the scope of this book. I am just making the point that society is active in deciding which issues really are problems, and sometimes problems disappear simply because we decide they are no longer problems.

What Should We Do Now?

With all this information about the condition of the world, what do we do with it? Potentially a lot of different things, but here are six implications that I could think of for how we live our lives. The first three concern how we think, the next three what we do.

(1) **Be aware of good news.** We hear a lot of bad news, so it's easy to overlook the many good things that are happening in the world. As former president Bill Clinton once said, tongue-in-cheek, we "have to face the fact that there is some good news on the landscape. We are going to have to learn to live with it."[22] Accepting this good news encourages us now, and it gives us energy to solve future problems. Our past successes can stimulate our future effort.[23]

We should be thankful for the blessings we've received. While we hear people thank God for their food, their healthy children, or even their job, when was the last time you heard someone thank God for the declining national crime rate? Or the rise in literacy around the world? Or the amazing decrease in poverty over the past generation? Aren't these things worth being thankful for?

217

(2) **Be skeptical of what you hear, especially negative news.** The converse of accepting the good news is being skeptical of the bad news. Many people in society have an incentive to exaggerate problems. They use bad news to increase ratings, gather donations, get votes, etc.... Even if this alarmism serves a purpose, which it might well do, it doesn't mean we have to accept it as true. We don't have to believe all that we hear. Critically evaluating bad news not only spares us from unnecessary fear and loathing, it also clarifies which problems really are getting worse. We should neither accept all wolf-cries nor reject the possible existence of a wolf. Instead, we should think for ourselves about whether danger is present and, if so, how we should respond.

(3) **Distinguish "is" from "ought."** Our society has visions for what life should be like. We also have information about how it is actually doing, and trouble arises when we confuse the two. In particular, we sometimes judge the world's condition only by the standard of what we want it to be, which, more often than not, leads to disappointment. Visions and aspirations make social progress possible, but they can also lead us to overlook the real progress that has been made. Instead, let's be fully aware of what has happened as well as what we want to happen.[24]

(4) **Match resources to problems.** Problem solving requires resources—time, effort, money, and attention—and we can use our resources most effectively when we have an accurate understanding of the problems of the world. We get the most "bang for the buck" by applying resources to more severe problems and those problems for which interventions might have the greatest impact. Basically, we should emphasize a cost-benefit approach to solving the world's problems—how to do the most good with the resources we have.

Some people have a knee-jerk reaction against "cost-benefit" analysis when it comes to serious social problems, as if rational analysis is inappropriate when it comes to alleviating suffering. A cost-benefit analysis is not a matter of saying some things—e.g., poverty, global health—cost too much to fix. Rather, it's acknowledging that our resources are finite. If we send a doctor to fight AIDS in Bangkok we can't also send her to fight malaria in Rwanda. So where will our time, attention, and charitable funds be most effective? In Christian terms, this is called good stewardship.

Various experts have produced cost-benefit analyses of world problems. For example, one study by public health researchers identified over five hundred ways to save lives, and it put a price tag on each one—how much it cost per one year of life saved.[25] The most cost-effective interventions included medical procedures. For instance, colon and cervical cancer screenings of at-risk people save a year of life for only several thousand dollars. Other interventions cost much, much more. Environmental regulations were among the most costly. For example, radon remediation in homes with lower levels of radon costs $140,000 per year of life saved.

Science writer Matt Ridley identifies four problems in developing countries that are both severe and easily preventable—hunger, dirty water, indoor smoke, and malaria. He makes a strong case that the world should focus on solving these problems.[26]

Political scientist and environmental-gadfly Bjorn Lomborg asks how we could best spend $10 billion to benefit the world. He suggests that we improve health and combat diseases rather than trying to fix climate change.[27] Regardless of whether you agree with any particular remedy, this way of thinking is the best way to approach the world's problems. What will do the most good for the least cost? Lomborg puts it well:

> To get the most bang for your buck—and ensure that your generosity does the greatest good for the

largest number of people—you will need to prioritize, weighing up the costs and benefits of different
options. Unfortunately, we too often focus on the
most fashionable spending options rather than the
most rational.[28]

(5) **Simplify, consume less.** Many of the world's problems
today stem from overconsumption. For much of history,
humans have struggled against scarcity—having enough
food, shelter, and clothing. Now most people, certainly here
in the United States, have that pretty much taken care of.
At this point in history we need to transition from external
constraints on consumption—such as having resources—to
internal constraints—saying no, that's enough, and I can
do without. In some ways, refusing to consume is more
difficult than acquiring more things to consume; however,
the road to progress is one of voluntary, rather than forced,
simplicity.

How do we pursue a simple life? You can find many practical suggestions online. Just search for the terms *voluntary
simplicity, radical simplicity,* or *downshifting.* Sociologist
Juliet Schor recommends the following strategies: distinguishing between needs and wants, finding support from
others, sharing rather than buying, not purchasing things
for every holiday and social occasion, spending more time
on meaningful activities, and supporting societal-level
changes toward simplicity.[29]

(6) **Entangle yourself in social relationships.** My final sugges-
tion is the opposite of simplicity. It's a call for complexity
and entanglement, but with people instead of things. Most
Americans have enough wealth that we can isolate ourselves
from others, or at least only deal with them when it's conve-
nient to us. I understand this. Social relationships are costly
in time and energy, so why not pick and choose what works
for us at the moment? Unfortunately this produces shallower,
less supportive relationships; and no, we can't compensate

for this with social network sites. Several hundred Facebook friends cannot replace close, face-to-face ties. There is no substitute for in-person, intentional relationships, which are messy, demanding, and ultimately life-giving.

I wish I could illustrate this relationships-first approach from my own life, but, well, at best I'm average in this area. I do, however, have some friends who have rearranged their lives to emphasize the importance of relationships, so I'll share some of their stories.

- Susan noticed that she would see friends and acquaintances when she was running errands, but because of work and family obligations she usually didn't have time to stop and talk with them. So she started leaving for errands fifteen to twenty minutes early so she could give people more time and attention.

- Amy has decided not to use Facebook. It's not that she's opposed to technology; rather, she wants to interact with people in deeper ways, whether by phone, face-to-face, or even e-mail.

- Marc had a friend who was hospitalized for an extended period. This man had a son who played on a local high school basketball team, so Marc went to the basketball games and texted a play-by-play account of the games to his friend.

The general point here is that we can make our lives richer with people as opposed to things, but this requires intentional time and effort. We can join groups, stay in taxing relationships, support others, and, in general, do for others what we'd like them to do for us. Social relationships, as we all know, can be messy, frustrating, and exhausting, but they make our world a better place in a way that consuming more money, things, calories, fossil fuel, and reality television never will.

Ultimately, the world is steadily getting better, and it will probably continue to do so with or without us. However, we can further improve the quality of our own lives by acknowledging this change for the better and contributing to it with stewardship of what we have, simplicity in how we live, and love for others.

NOTES

Chapter 1: Pessimism About Our Nation and World

1. His nom de plume.

2. CBS News/*New York Times* poll, January 2009.

3. Surveys have asked this question periodically since 1986. In the late 1980s, more respondents said "getting better" than "getting worse." Since 1991, however, the "getting worse" responses have outnumbered the "getting better" by at least 2 to 1.

4. In many years, this question was asked multiple times. In those years, I took data from only one survey, choosing the one collected nearest to April 1 of that year—a date chosen for no particular reason.

5. Hunter and Bowman, 1996.

6. I listed these areas of life in decreasing order of negativity, with moral standards being perceived as in the most decline and racial issues in the least decline (relatively speaking).

7. Guzman et al., 2003.

8. Pew Research Center, 2010, 33.

9. The Pew Research Center has asked this question since 2002, and every year the majority of respondents in nearly every country were dissatisfied with the way things were going in their country.

10. Cited in Whitman, 1998, 115.

11. Pew Research Center, 2006.

12. Summarized in Samuelson, 1995, 52.

13. In many, but not all, of the years, about twice as many respondents described their financial situation as getting better than as getting worse.

14. Saad, 2007.

15. Hayward, 2008, 13. Education and government officials, Best, 2004, 89. Moral standards to health care, Whitman, vii.

16. Quotation taken from Whitman, 14.

17. Whitman, 61; Stone, 2009.

18. Whitman, 61.

19. CBS News/*New York Times* poll, January 2009.

20. Pew Research Center for the People & the Press, 2009.

21. CBS News/*New York Times* poll, March 2008 and January 2009.

22. Gallup/*USA Today* Poll, January 2010. I thank David Weakliem for pointing me to these data, and yes, David, you were right.

23. Pew Research Center, 2006a.

24. Ibid., 2006b.

25. By the way, I'm kind of proud that I know this word.

26. Some of Ehrlich's proposed solutions are also difficult to accept. He raised the possibility of adding birth-control substances to the water or food supply; increased taxes on larger families and baby-related materials such as diapers and cribs; and a governmental agency to identify and encourage the nation's ideal population size.

27. Cited by Moore and Simon, 2000, 20.

28. Lomborg, 2001, 61.

29. Ehrlich, 1968.

30. Goklany, 2007.

31. Ehrlich and Ehrlich, 1974.

32. Goeller, 1995.

33. Ehrlich, 1970.

34. World Almanac, 2010, 174.

35. Ehrlich, 1968.

36. Easterbrook, 2003, 42–3.

37. Ehrlich, 1968.

38. His nom de plume.

39. Council on Environmental Quality, 1980, 1.

40. Kaplan, 1994.

41. Garrett,1994, quoted in Easterbrook, 103.

42. Gerald Celente, cited by Lindgreen, 2009.

43. Whitman, 119.

44. Glassner, 1999, xviii.

45. Lomborg, 2004, 22.

46. Whitman, 119.

47. Ibid., viii.

48. Lomborg, 14.

49. *www.mayoclinic.com/health/positive-thinking/SR00009*

50. Arehart-Treiche, 2007.

51. Clearly there is variation among Christians in their definition of social problems; the approach taken in this book is not meant to represent Christians as a whole but rather to simply reflect my own, limited understanding of the faith.

52. World Almanac, 2010, 150.

53. Lomborg, 2001, 4, makes this point about examining change.

54. Quoted in Whitman, 83.

55. Samuelson, 1995, xv.

Chapter 2: Why Are We So Sure Things Are Going Downhill?

1. Quoted in Whitman, 9.

2. Wattenberg, 1984, 371.

3. Lomborg, 2004, 30.

4. Many others have made this point, e.g., Glassner, 1999; Best, 2001; Wattenberg.

5. Former *Wall Street Journal* bureau chief Amanda Bennett suggests that reporters and writers may not be able to write positive stories even if they want to. Based on what she calls the template theory, editors and other people who aren't actually on the scene make a decision about what "the story" is, and they in turn guide what is to be reported on and published, e.g., the story in China before Tiananmen Square was good news about a post-Mao China, a good country getting better. With Tiananmen Square, the template reversed, and now it's only stories about human rights abuses. In both cases, reporters complained that stories contrary to the template don't make the papers. Murray, Schwartz, and Lichter, 2001, 29.

6. Ibid., 17.

7. Hayward, 2008, 19.

8. A 1983 study by Holmes Brown of Applied Economics, described in Wattenberg, 373.

9. Whitman, ix.

10. Wattenberg, 112.

11. Ibid., 19.

12. Garte, 2008, 13, makes this point forcibly.

13. Rossi, 1987.

14. *The Economist*, 79, May 29, 2010.

15. Best, 2001, 2.

16. Lomborg 2004, 21.

17. This example is taken from Ridley, 2010, 290.

18. Garte, 2007, viii.

19. Whitman, 6–7.

20. Best, 2004, 4, 6.

21. Myers, 2000, xiii.

22. *http://nces.ed.gov/programs/digest/d09/tables/dt09_034.asp*

23. *www.snopes.com/language/document/school.asp*

24. Best, 2001.

25. This example is drawn from Best, 2001, 62–64.

26. Hoff Sommers, 1995.

27. Lomborg, 2001, 23.

28. Whitman, vii.

29. Cox and Alm, 1999, 200.

30. John Mueller, quoted by Whitman, 7.

31. Whitman, 7.

32. Quotation from Moore and Simon, 2000, 21.

33. Quotation from Samuelson, 1995, 14.

34. Ibid., 4.

35. Ibid.

36. Ibid., 141.

37. Ibid., 50.

38. Easterbrook, xvi.

39. I hesitate to give specific examples of Christian leaders doing this because I don't want to target any one person as doing this, and I know of no systematic analysis of this type of data. However, this assertion fits well with my own experiences as a sermon-listening, book-reading Christian for several decades now.

40. Quoted from Boyer, 1992, 333.

41. Ibid.

Chapter 3: Are We Worse Off Financially Than We Used to Be?

1. Fischer and Hout, 2006, 139–140.

2. Samuelson, 1995, 7.

3. Economic Report to the President, 2010, 7.

4. They wrote this in 1999. Since then, the economy has gone through various changes, but their characterization appears still to be true.

5. This figure replicates Figure 8.3 in the 2010 Economic Report to the President. The dollar measure is in 2008 dollars, meaning that it adjusts for inflation. As such, the income reported in earlier years is not what people actually earned in that year, but rather what it was worth in terms of today's dollars.

6. Department of Commerce (Census Bureau), Income, Poverty, and Health Insurance Coverage in the United States Table A-2; Current Population Survey, Annual Social and Economic Supplement, Historical Income Table F-12.

7. Economic Report to the President, 218.

8. Also, our nation's economy experienced slower productivity growth, and the progress was less for poorer families—two more factors for why family incomes slowed down. Ibid., 33.

9. Ibid., 218.

10. Cox and Alm, 18.

11. Sowell, 2008, 131.

12. Pew Research Center, 2008.

13. Ibid.

14. Reynolds, 2006, 68.

15. Sowell, 132.

16. 2001.

17. Sowell, 78.

18. There is also substantial income variation by race and ethnicity. In 2008, Asian households had a median income of $65,000, whites $56,000, Hispanics $38,000, and African-Americans $35,000. This difference, like the gender difference, is diminishing over time—at least for native-born Americans. Pew Research Center, 2008; DeNavas-Walt, Proctor, and Smith, 2009.

19. "Gross national income per capita 2009, Atlas method and PPP." World Development Indicators database, World Bank, revised 9 July 2010. Purchasing Power Parity in International Dollars.

20. Goklany, 2007, 42.

21. Ibid., 40.

22. Maddison, 2007, 29.

23. Ridley, 14, notes that during this time, real income per capita decreased in only six countries: Afghanistan, Haiti, Congo, Liberia, Sierra Leone, and Somalia.

24. Bachelor taxes still exist. We just call them tax deductions for marriage and children.

25. Maddison.

26. *http://partnersworldwide.org*

27. Further highlighting the arbitrary—and often political—nature of poverty, the officials actually developed two poverty thresholds, and President Johnson and his advisors chose the lower threshold. Beeghley, 1984.

28. Caplow, Hicks, and Wattenberg, 2001, 174.

29. DeNavas-Walt, Proctor, and Smith, 2008.

30. Rector, 1995, 252.

31. Best, 2001, 51.

32. Sowell, 129.

33. Cox and Alm, 14.

34. Caplow, Hicks, and Wattenberg, 174.

35. U.S. Census Bureau, Current Population Survey, 1960 to 2009 Annual Social and Economic Supplements. Reprinted in DeNavas-Walt, Proctor, and Smith, 2008.

36. Plotnick et al., 2000, 265.

37. Becker, 2004, 62.

38. Federal Interagency Forum on Child and Family Statistics, 2009.

39. Reynolds, 2006, 31.

40. Easterbrook, 54. As a caveat, poverty can affect education, marriage, and childbearing as well, so the causality isn't only in one direction.

41. When considering worldwide poverty, it's worth noting that much, if not most, of the economic activity in developing countries happens "off the books," in the informal

economic sector. As such, official measures of poverty underestimate true income, so it's difficult to precisely compare poverty levels across countries. Sowell, 198.

42. Data drawn from Chen and Ravallion, 2008.

43. Ridley, 15.

44. *www.hopeinternational.org*

45. Fischer and Hout, 137. See also Wilkinson and Pickett, 2009.

46. Burtless and Jencks, 2002.

47. Ibid.

48. Data from DeNavas-Walt, Proctor, and Smith, 2008. Measured in 2008 dollars.

49. It's worth noting that the increase in income did not happen in a linear manner. For example, since 1995, the average income of the bottom fifth has actually decreased slightly.

50. Piketty and Saez, 2001.

51. Ibid.

52. Sowell, 127.

53. Fischer and Hout, 119; Becker, 2004, 57.

54. Morris and Western, 1999.

55. Easterbrook, 10.

56. Fischer and Hout, 119.

57. Ridley, 18.

58. Morris and Western, 1999; Burtless and Jencks.

59. Here's the technical definition of the Gini index, quoted from the 2010 CIA World Factbook: "This index measures the degree of inequality in the distribution of family income in a country. The index is calculated from the Lorenz curve, in which cumulative family income is plotted against the number of families arranged from the poorest to the richest. The index is the ratio of (a) the area between a country's Lorenz curve and the 45-degree helping line to (b) the entire triangular area under the 45-degree line. The more nearly equal a country's income distribution, the closer its Lorenz curve to the 45-degree line and the lower its Gini index. The more unequal a country's income distribution, the farther its Lorenz curve from the 45-degree line and the higher its Gini index. If income were distributed with perfect equality, the Lorenz curve would coincide with the 45-degree line and the index would be 0; if income were distributed with perfect inequality, the Lorenz curve would coincide with the horizontal axis and the right vertical axis and the index would be 100."

60. Data taken from the 2009 U.N. Human Development Report.

61. *www.urban-ministry.com/*

62. Becker, 2004, 33.

63. U.S. Bureau of Labor Statistics, Bulletin 2307; and *Employment and Earnings*, monthly. Data for 1947 and earlier apply to age fourteen and older. Data for year 2010 are only for the first six months.

64. Fischer and Hout, 129; Caplow, Hicks, and Wattenberg, 46.

65. Fischer and Hout, 128.

66. Keyssar, 1995, 198.

67. Cox and Alm, 39–40.

68. Lomborg, 2001, 62.

69. Cox and Alm.

70. Ibid., 40.

71. Despite falling food prices, 76% of Americans reported in an April 2008 Gallup poll that rising food prices are a crisis or major problem.

72. Ridley, 23.

73. Ibid., 22.

74. Cox and Alm, 19.

75. Ibid., 26

76. Easterbrook, 96.

77. Cox and Alm, 14.

78. Ibid., 14.

79. Easterbrook, 96.

80. Pew Research Center, 2008.

81. Cox and Alm, 42.

82. Caplow, Hicks, and Wattenberg; Economic Report to the President, 121.

83. This isn't actually true, though it makes for a good jingle. McDonald's in India replaced the Big Mac with the Chicken Maharaja-Mac. In Saudi Arabia the Big Mac is made with lamb. *www.trifter.com/practical-travel/budget-travel/mcdonald's-strange-menu-around-the-world/*

84. *www.economist.com/markets/Bigmac/index.cfm*

85. Hoefert and Hofer, 2006.

86. U.S. Department of Commerce: Bureau of Economic Analysis. Data taken from January each year. *www.bea.gov/national/pdf/nipaguid.pdf*

87. Garner, 2006.

88. Economic Report to the President, 117.

89. E.g., *www.timesrecordnews.com/news/2009/jun/07/family-pet-gets-credit-card-job-offers-in-mail/* Accessed January 3, 2011.

90. *www.federalreserve.gov/releases/housedebt/*

91. Pew Research Center, 2008.

Chapter 4: Are We Dumber Than We Used to Be?

1. Cited in Easterbrook, 55.

2. Lemann, 2010.

3. Flynn, 1987, 189.

4. Crissey, 2009.

5. Miringoff and Miringoff, 1999, 57.

6. U.S. Census Bureau, Current Population Reports, P20–536; and "Years of School

Completed by People 25 Years Old and Over, by Age and Sex: Selected Years 1940 to 2002."
www.census.gov/population/www/socdemo/educ-attn.html

7. Economic Report to the President, 36.

8. Becker, 2004, 67.

9. We each spent five years in college, and I took seven years for my PhD while she spent nine on hers.

10. Caplow, Hicks, and Wattenberg, 56.

11. U.S. Census Bureau, U.S. Census of Population, 1960, 1970, and 1980, Vol. 1; and Current Population Reports, P20–550, and earlier reports; *www.census.gov/population/www/socdemo/educ-attn.html*

12. Fischer and Hout, 17.

13. Maddison, 1995; 1998.

14. UNESCO, 2007.

15. Ibid.

16. Ibid.

17. Ibid., 80.

18. *www.berea.edu*

19. Ibid., 84.

20. U.S. Department of Commerce, Bureau of the Census, Historical Statistics of the United States, Colonial Times to 1970; and Current Population Reports, Series P-23, Ancestry and Language in the United States: November 1979.

21. UNESCO, 2007.

22. Ibid., 258.

23. Lomborg, 2001, 81.

24. Easterbrook; UNESCO, 258.

25. *www.christianliteracy.com*

26. Easterlin, 2000.

27. Gardner.

28. Tiefenthaler, 2009.

29. Rampey, Dion, and Donahue, 2009. The format of the National Assessment of Educational Progress (NAEP) was changed in 2004, hence two different data points: one representing the prior form of measurement, and the second showing the current form.

30. Ibid., 5.

31. World Almanac, 2010, 394–395.

32. "In 1995, the College Board recentered the scoring scale for the SAT by reestablishing the original mean score of 500 on the 200–800 scale. The data presented here are adjusted to account for this recentering." World Almanac, 395.

33. This description of Flynn's findings is summarized from Gladwell, 2007.

34. Holloway, 1999.

Chapter 5: Are We Sicker Than We Used to Be?

1. Quoted in Moore and Simon, 2000, 26.
2. Easterbrook, xiv.
3. Joint United Nations Programme on HIV/AIDS, 2008, 11.
4. World Almanac; National Vital Statistics Reports, Vol. 58, No. 21, June 28, 2010.
5. Data for race and gender differences from the National Vital Statistics Report.
6. Blue, 2008.
7. Strow and Strow, 2006.
8. National Vital Statistics Reports, Table 1.
9. This discussion is summarized from Fischer and Hout, 63.
10. Preston, 1995, 30.
11. Hatcher, 1986.
12. Hollingsworth, 1977.
13. Goklany, 2007, 34.
14. World Health Organization, 2009.
15. Ridley, 14.
16. Oeppen and Vaupel, 2002, 1031.
17. *www.mercyships.org*
18. Dennis Wrong, quoted in Miringoff and Miringoff, 1999; Federal Interagency Forum on Child and Family Statistics 2009.
19. Maddison, 2007, 31; Simon, 1995.
20. Worldwide infant morality rates drawn from Goklany, 2007, 28.
21. Ridley, 14; Goklany, 2007, 31.
22. Goklany, 2007, 29–30.
23. World Health Organization, 2009.
24. UNESCO, 35.
25. *www.haitianhealthfoundation.org*
26. Haines, 1995, 51.
27. Historical Statistics of the United States, Series B291–304.
28. National Cancer Institute, 2006.
29. Edwards et al., 2009.
30. National Cancer Institute, 2006.
31. Centers for Disease Control and Prevention, 2010.
32. Ibid., 2009.
33. Ibid., 2010.
34. Ibid.
35. Joint United Nations Programme on HIV/AIDS, 2008.
36. Ibid.
37. *www.cmmb.org*
38. Lomborg, 2001, 57.

39. Caplow, Hicks, and Wattenberg, 144.

40. Moore and Simon, 2000, 209.

41. Ibid.

42. World Health Organization, 2009.

43. National Institute on Alcohol Abuse and Alcoholism, 2010, *www.niaaa.nih.gov/ Resources/DatabaseResources/QuickFacts/AlcoholSales/Pages/consum02.aspx* Accessed August 22, 2010.

44. Organisation for Economic Co-operation and Development (OECD) Health Data, 2005, *www.nationmaster.com/graph/foo_alc_con-food-alcohol-consumption-current* Accessed August 12, 2010.

45. World Health Organization, 2009.

46. National Center for Health Statistics, 2010, 284.

47. Wang, 2006; Easterbrook.

48. Panagopoulos, 2006

49. Wang.

50. Panagopoulos.

51. A sentence written for myself as much as anyone.

52. Federal Interagency Forum on Child and Family Statistics, 2009.

53. National Center for Health Statistics, 2010.

54. Data from OECD, 2005, *www.nationmaster.com/graph/hea_obe-health-obesity* Accessed 8/16/10.

55. Ibid.

56. Food and Agriculture Organization of the United Nations, 2000, 6.

57. World Almanac, 2010, 735.

58. Food and Agriculture Organization of the United Nations, 2000; 2009.

59. Lomborg, 2001, 61.

60. Maddison, 2007.

61. Goklany, 2002.

62. Lomborg, 2001, 63

63. Grantham, 1995, 373.

64. Avery, 1995, 380.

65. Goklany, 2009c.

66. *www.gleanings.org*

67. World Almanac, 172.

68. Caplow, Hicks, and Wattenberg, 236.

69. World Almanac, 173; National Safety Council.

70. Caplow, Hicks, and Wattenberg, 237.

71. Ibid., 236.

72. World Almanac, 94.

73. Moore and Simon, 2000, 140.

74. World Almanac, 173.

75. Moore and Simon, 2000, 172.

76. Easterbrook, 50.

77. Cox and Alm, 65.

78. Ibid.

79. Much of the increase in poisonings comes from accidental overdoses of prescription drugs. Fackelmann, 2008.

80. Example and data from Ridley, 335.

81. Goklany, 2009c.

82. National Center for Health Statistics, 2010, Table 26.

83. Xu et al., 2010.

84. Data from National Center for Health Statistics, presented in World Almanac, 174.

Chapter 6: Are We Stressed and Unhappy?

1. Carroll, 2007.

2. Cited in Whitman, 35.

3. 1997, xvi.

4. Data drawn from multiple Gallup poll surveys via the Roper Center's iPoll database. This pattern of happiness—modestly increasing in recent years—has been found with other survey measures of happiness as well, making it a more reliable finding.

5. Veenhoven and Hagerty, 2006.

6. Stone, et al., 2010.

7. Easterbrook, 169.

8. Stone.

9. Deaton, 2008.

10. Ibid., 4. In statistical terms, there's a linear relationship between the life satisfaction and the log of income.

11. Inglehart et al., 2008.

12. Ibid.

13. Ibid.

14. Van Praag and Fijters, 1999.

15. Myers, 2000, 133.

16. Brooks, 2008, 118.

17. Lane, 2000, 73.

18. Kahneman and Deaton, 2010.

19. Inglehart et al.

20. Kahneman and Deaton.

21. This description of Platt is taken from Brooks, 2010.

22. I write this as a stone-cold hypocrite because I do nothing of the sort. My wife and I are paying off substantial amounts of educational and consumer debt, resulting from both

good and bad decisions, and though we're making more than $75,000 a year, we're nowhere near giving much of it away. File this paragraph in the "Do as I say, not as I do" folder.

23. *www.resurrectionband.com*

24. Suicide is difficult to measure, for it depends on how law enforcement officials explain a death. Some suicides, especially when a note is left behind, are straightforward. Others, however, might be accidents. For example, it's difficult to know whether some drownings, falls, and self-shootings are intentional. Sometimes family members cover up a suicide out of embarrassment or to secure insurance benefits. Best, 2001, 23.

25. National Center for Health Statistics, 2010, 240.

26. Washington University in St. Louis, 1998.

27. *www.afsp.org/index.cfm*

28. World Health Organization, *www.who.int/mental_health/prevention/suicide /suicideprevent/en/* Accessed August 30, 2010.

29. Ibid.

30. World Health Organization, 2002.

31. *www.mercyministries.org*

32. Cox and Alm, 54.

33. Ausubel and Grubler, 1995, 201.

34. Some analyzsts, such as Schor, 1992, have argued that the workweek increased substantially in the last half of the twentieth century, but few economists accept this conclusion, citing problems with the data analyzed by Schor. Whaples, 2001; Jacobs and Gerson, 2001.

35. Fischer and Hout, 122; Costa, 2000.

36. Cox and Alm, 55.

37. Fischer and Hout, 122.

38. Whaples, 2001.

39. Coontz, 1992, 11.

40. Ibid., 13.

41. Fischer and Hout, 105.

42. Ibid., 124.

43. Hout and Hanley, 2002.

44. Ibid.

45. Berry, 2007.

46. Robinson and Godbey, 2005, 413.

47. Cited in Easterbrook, 29.

48. Aguiar and Hurst, 2007.

49. John Robinson, cited by Easterbrook, 2003.

50. Bianchi et al., 2000.

51. Ibid.

52. Lomborg, 2001, 79.

53. Robert Putnam, 1997, xv.

54. Robinson and Godbey.

55. Jacobs and Gerson, 2001.

56. Goodin et al., 2005

57. This discussion is adapted from Goodin et al.

58. Bureau of Labor Statistics, American Time Use Survey, June 10, 2010.

59. This includes 35.5 hours of traditional television and 2 hours of time-shifted (e.g., recorded) television. Nielsen Company, 2010a.

60. Nielsen Company, 2010b.

61. Rideout, Foehr, and Roberts, 2010, 4.

62. Dye and Johnson, 2009, 2.

63. Myers, 197.

64. Ibid., 199.

65. Whitman, 32.

66. Myers, 196.

67. Ibid., 198.

68. Whitman, 31.

69. Dye and Johnson, 7.

Chapter 7: What About Crime and War, Freedom and Faith?

1. Pew Center on the States, 2008, 5.

2. Saad, 2007, 1.

3. Freedom House, 2009, 3.

4. Caplow, Hicks, and Wattenberg, 214. Of course, there can be ambiguity as to the causes of death or whether a death has occurred.

5. Historical Statistics of the United States, Colonial Times to 1970; Mini-Historical Statistics from Statistical Abstract, 2003; Statistical Abstract of the United States, 2010.

6. Statistical Abstract of the United States, 2010, Table 295.

7. Ibid., Tables 300 and 301.

8. Ibid., Table 295.

9. Caplow, Hicks, and Wattenberg, 220.

10. Becker, 2004, 75.

11. Donohue III and Levitt, 2001.

12. For example, Foote and Goetz, 2005, claim that Donohue and Levitt incorrectly specified their regression models. Joyce, 2004, argued that legalized abortions simply replaced prior illegal abortions. Donohue and Levitt have responded to these critiques, standing by their original hypothesis.

13. Statistical Abstract of the United States, 2010; United Nations Office on Drugs and Crime, 2009.

14. European Institute for Crime Prevention and Control, 2010.

15. United Nations Office on Drugs and Crime, 2009.

16. Ibid.

17. Geneva Declaration, 2008, 67.

18. European Institute for Crime Prevention and Control, 2010, 18.

19. Spierenburg, 2008, 4.

20. Ibid., 223.

21. *www.rawhide.org*

22. World Almanac, 126.

23. Note that analysts vary in how they compute imprisonment rates. Some count those in prisons and local jails, others just prisons. Others calculate the rate using the number of adults in a particular country, while others use the entire population. Because of this, the numbers in this section vary somewhat depending on the source.

24. Historical Statistics of the United States, Colonial Times to 1970; Mini-Historical Statistics from Statistical Abstract, 2003; Statistical Abstract, 2010.

25. Caplow, Hicks, and Wattenberg, 222.

26. Ibid., 225.

27. Sabol, West, and Cooper, 2008.

28. Walmsley, 2008.

29. Pew Center on the States, 2008.

30. Ibid.

31. Pager, 2003. The 50% figure refers to white job applicants.

32. *www.prisonfellowship.org*

33. There are several types of war-related deaths. Combatant deaths are the number of military personnel who die in battles. Battle deaths are all people who die in combat, both military and civilians. War deaths, the broadest category, includes all battle deaths plus indirectly caused deaths such as famine, disease, genocides, and increased criminal violence. The middle measure—battle deaths—has been suggested to be the best measure of the scale and scope of military operations, so that is what I use here. Human Security Report Project, 2009.

34. Ibid.

35. Lacina and Gleditsch, 2005.

36. *www.persecutionproject.org*

37. *http://academic.udayton.edu/race/02rights/jcrow02.htm*

38. Thernstrom and Thernstrom, 1997, 44.

39. Bertrand and Mullainathan, 2004.

40. Political rights include the freedom to vote in legitimate elections, compete for public office, join political parties, and elect representatives who are accountable to the electorate. Civil liberties include the freedom of expression and belief, freedom to associate with others of one's own choosing, the rule of law, and personal autonomy without undue interference from the state. Freedom House, 2010.

41. Inglehart, 2008.

42. Garte, 2008, xiii.

43. UNESCO, 2007.

44. Freedom House, 2010.

45. Ibid.

46. Freedom House, summarized by Simon and Moore, 2000, 257.

47. Goklany, 2001

48. *World Ark* magazine. Holiday 2010, 45.

49. Pew Forum on Religion and Public Life, 2008.

50. Finke and Stark, 1992. Their concept of "adherence" incorporates both affiliation and involvement.

51. Barrett, Kurian, and Johnson, 2001.

52. Ibid.

53. Since Islam is the smaller religion, this equates to a greater increase percentagewise. Note: The increase in adherents is a function of multiple processes, including births, deaths, conversions, and deconversions.

54. Barrett, Kurian, and Johnson, 2001.

55. *www.wycliffe.org*

Chapter 8: What About Marriage and Families?

1. National Marriage Project, 2009, 88.

2. 2007.

3. 2008.

4. Strow and Strow, 2006.

5. Once again, these correlations are open to multiple interpretations. Perhaps the kinds of people who get divorced would have these problems anyway, or perhaps divorce causes these problems. Presumably both dynamics are at play, but sociologists associate divorce with negative outcomes even when using multivariate analyses to take personal and family differences into account.

6. Bramlett and Mosher, 2001, 2; Myers, 43.

7. Cited in Myers, 43.

8. National Marriage Project, 2009.

9. Summarized in National Marriage Project.

10. Wilcox, 2009.

11. National Marriage Project.

12. Historical Statistics of the United States, Colonial Times to 1970, Series B 216–220; Statistical Abstract of the United States, 1999.

13. Fischer and Hout, 71.

14. Myers, 52.

15. Whitman, 88.

16. Strow and Strow.

17. The World Almanac 2010.

18. Fischer and Hout, 71.

19. Myers, 39.

20. Mosher, Chandra, and Jones, 2005.

21. Myers, 48.

22. *www.oecd.org/els/social/family/database*

23. Levine, et al., 1995.

24. Meisner, Bob, Audrey Meisner, and Stephen W. Nance. 2004. *Marriage Undercover: Thriving in a Culture of Quiet Desperation.* Newburg, PA: MileStones International Publishers.

25. Certainly some children are better off in one-parent families, when it means removing them from physical or substance abuse. The evidence covered here regards the average differences between children in one- and two-parent families.

26. Myers, 73.

27. Ibid., 76–80.

28. Bramlett and Mosher, 2001.

29. Myers, 117.

30. Ibid., 78.

31. Ibid., 85.

32. Ibid., 76.

33. U.S. Census Bureau, Current Population Survey, March and Annual Social and Economic Supplements, 2009 and earlier.

34. World Almanac, 168.

35. U.S. Census Bureau, Current Population Survey, March and Annual Social and Economic Supplements, 2009 and earlier.

36. Becker, 2004, 7.

37. Pew Research Center, 2007, 3.

38. Fischer and Hout, 81.

39. Ibid., 80.

40. Pew Research Center, 2007, 15.

41. *www.loveincecc.org*

42. Gauthier, Smeedeng, and Furstenberg, 2004.

43. Dye and Johnson, 2009.

44. Caplow, Hicks, and Wattenberg, 88.

45. Sayer, Bianchi, Robinson, 2004.

46. Dye and Johnson.

47. Sayer, Bianchi, Robinson.

48. Gauthier, Smeedeng, and Furstenberg.

49. Cohabitation is measured as two unmarried people of the opposite sex living together in a sexual relationship.

50. Pew Research Center, 2007.

51. Ibid.

52. Smock, 2000.

53. Ibid., 3.

54. Pew Research Center, 2007, 33.

55. Smock.

56. Ibid., 6; Myers, 29.

57. Gallup/*USA Today* poll, July 2008.

58. Myers, 30; Smock.

59. Caplow, Hicks, and Wattenberg, 72.

60. Federal Interagency Forum on Child and Family Statistics, 2009.

61. Myers, 19.

62. Finer, 2007. He defines premarital sex as either having had vaginal intercourse before first marrying or ever having had intercourse and never having married.

63. Summarized in Wattenberg, 1984, 293.

64. Analysis of "everstray" variable since year 2000.

65. Mosher, Chandra, and Jones, 2005.

66. Guttmacher Institute, 2010.

67. National Center for Health Statistics, 2010.

68. Jones, Finer, and Singh, 2010.

69. Fischer and Hout, 224–225.

70. CBS News Poll, August 2010.

71. Fischer and Hout, 224–225.

72. Guttmacher Institute, 2009.

73. *www.adoptionbychoice.org*. This and several other stories of "Christians making a difference" was found in a [1997] 2007 issue of *Christianity Today* that featured "100 things the church is doing right."

Chapter 9: What About the Environment?

1. 2004

2. 2004, xxii.

3. Lomborg, 2001, 31.

4. Whitman, 68.

5. Lomborg, 2001, 3.

6. Worldwatch Institute, 2003.

7. Lomborg, 2001, 3.

8. Hayward and Kaleita, 2007, 30.

9. Lomborg, 2004, 14.

10. Gallup poll, March 2010.

11. Jones, 2010.

12. This background on Lomborg is drawn from the preface of *The Skeptical Environmentalist*.

13. *http://online.wsj.com/article/0,,SB107170224457630700,00.html*

14. Cited in Lomborg, 2004, 1.

15. Environmental Protection Agency, 2000.

16. Ridley, 304.

17. *Affluent Society*, cited in Moore and Simon, 2000.

18. Hayward and Kaleita, 2007, 39.

19. Environmental Protection Agency, 2000.

20. Federal Interagency Forum on Child and Family Statistics, 2009.

21. Lomborg, 2001, 171.

22. This discussion of the ozone layer is taken from Lomborg, 2001, 274.

23. U.S. Environmental Protection Agency, 2008.

24. Elsom, 1995, 477.

25. Reported in Hayward, 2009, 24.

26. Committee on Transportation and Infrastructure, 2008.

27. Goklany, 153.

28. Lebergott, 1995, 150.

29. Goklany, 153.

30. Gleick et al., 2009.

31. United Nations, 2010, 58.

32. Support International, *http://supportintl.org/cleanwater.aspx*

33. *www.water.cc*

34. Food and Agriculture Organization of the United Nations, 2005, 16.

35. This discussion is adapted from Sedjo and Clawson, 1995, 331.

36. *www.nationalatlas.gov/articles/biology/a_forest.html*

37. Ibid.

38. Easterbrook, 109.

39. Lomborg, 2001, 117.

40. Food and Agriculture Organization of the United Nations, 2005.

41. Food and Agriculture Organization of the United Nations, 2010.

42. Lomborg, 2001, 123.

43. Hayward, 2007, 39.

44. Food and Agriculture Organization of the United Nations, 2010, 6.

45. Ibid., Table 4.

46. Ridley, 144.

47. Rainforest Action Network, 2010.

48. *www.targetearth.org*

49. Environmental Protection Agency, 2010.

50. Goklany, 2009a.

51. Ibid., 2009b.

52. The Worldwatch Institute, 2009.

53. Goklany, 2009a.

54. Ridley, 341, 342.

55. Lomborg, 2001, 4.

56. United States Senate Committee on Environment and Public Works, 2006.

57. Cited in Moore and Simon, 2000, 184.

58. Environmental quality doesn't always increase linearly with wealth. For example, some types of air pollution show a U-shaped relationship. The poorest countries have insufficient manufacturing to produce air pollution, and the wealthiest countries have relatively clean manufacturing. It's the countries in the middle, with dirty manufacturing, that emit the most air pollution. Yandle et al., 2004.

59. Hayward, 2008, 4.

60. Anderson, 2004, xviii.

61. Hollander, 2003, makes this case convincingly.

Chapter 10: The Counting of Blessings

1. 1995, 6.

2. 2003, 80.

3. Taken from his 1950 Nobel Prize acceptance speech.

4. This thought experiment is adapted from Easterbrook, 82.

5. Opdycke and Miringoff, 2008.

6. Simon, 1995, 7.

7. Ibid., 7.

8. Ridley, 281.

9. Ibid., 282. He notes that this may be an apocryphal story.

10. Simon, quoted in Lomborg, 2001.

11. Ridley, 35.

12. Moore and Simon, 2000.

13. Goklany, 2004, 72.

14. Herper and Kang, 2006.

15. *www.xprize.org* Accessed December 3, 2010.

16. *http://archives.citypaper.net/articles/2009/03/12/the-simple-way-kensington-philadelphia*

17. List of advocates from Garte, 2008, xi.

18. *http://obf.cancer.gov/financial/factbook.htm* Accessed December 31, 2010.

19. Etzioni, 1993.

20. McPherson, Smith-Lovin, and Brashears, 2006. In 1985, three-fourths of Americans

said they had a friend in whom they could confide, but in 2004 the number had dropped to one-half.

21. Putnam, 2000.
22. Quoted in Whitman, 131.
23. Garte 2008, xii.
24. This distinction is drawn from Lomborg, 2004, 3, who traces it to Hume.
25. Tengs et al., 1995.
26. Ridley, 338.
27. Lomborg, 2008.
28. Lomborg.
29. Schor, 1999.

REFERENCES

America's Children. 2009. *America's Children: Key National Indicators of Well-Being,* 2009.

Anderson, Terry L. 2004. *You Have to Admit It's Getting Better: From Economic Prosperity to Environmental Quality.* Stanford, CA: Hoover Institution Press.

Aquiar, Mark, and Erik Hurst. 2007. "Measuring Trends in Leisure: The Allocation of Time over Five Decades." *The Quarterly Journal of Economics* 122(3): 969–1006.

Arehart-Treichel, Joan. 2007. "Negative Outlook on Life May Predispose to Cognitive Impairment." *Psychiatric News* 42(14): 27.

Ausubel, Jesse H., and Arnulf Grubler. 1995. "Working Less and Living Longer: Long-Term Trends in Working Time and Time Budgets." *Technological Forecasting and Social Change* 50: 195–213.

Avery, Dennis. 1995. "The World's Rising Food Productivity." *The State of Humanity,* 376–393, edited by Julian L. Simon. Oxford: Blackwell.

Barrett, David A, George T. Kurian, and Todd M. Johnson. 2001. *World Christian Encyclopedia.* Oxford: Oxford University Press.

Becker, Patricia C. 2004. *Social Change in America: The Historic Handbook 2004.* Blue Ridge Summit, PA: Bernan Press.

Beeghley, Leonard. 1984. "Illusion and Reality in the Measurement of Poverty." *Social Problems* 31(3): 322–333.

Berry, Brent. 2007. "Disparities in Free Time Inactivity in the United States: Trends and Explanations." *Sociological Perspectives* 50(2): 177–208.

Bertrand, Marianne, and Kevin F. Hallock. 2001. "The Gender Gap in Top Corporate Jobs." *Industrial and Labor Relations Review* 55(1): 3–21.

Bertrand, Marianne, and Sendhil Mullainathan. 2004. "Are Emily and Greg More

Employable than Lakisha and Jamal? A Field Experiment on Labor Market Discrimination." *American Economic Review* 94(4): 991–1013.

Best, Joel. 2001. *Damned Lies and Statistics: Untangling Numbers from the Media, Politicians, and Activists.* Berkeley: University of California Press.

Best, Joel. 2004. *More Damned Lies and Statistics: How Numbers Confuse Public Issues.* Berkeley: University of California Press.

Bianchi, Suzanne M., Melissa A. Milkie, Liana C. Sayer, and John P. Robinson. 2000. "Is Anyone Doing the Housework? Trends in the Gender Division of Household Labor." *Social Forces* 79(1): 191–228.

Blue, Laura. 2009. "Why Do Women Live Longer than Men?" *Time*, August 6, 2008.

Boyer, Paul. 1992. *When Time Shall Be No More: Prophecy Belief in Modern American Culture.* Cambridge, MA: Belknap Press.

Bramlett, Matthew D., and William D. Mosher. 2001. "First Marriage Dissolution, Divorce, and Remarriage: United States." *Advance Data from Vital and Health Statistics* No. 323. Hyattsville, MD: National Center for Health Statistics.

Brooks, Arthur C. 2008. *Gross National Happiness.* New York: Basic Books.

Brooks, David. 2010. "The Gospel of Wealth." *New York Times*, September 6, 2010.

Brownback, Sam. 2008. "A Family Crisis." *New York Times* Op-Ed, March 2, 2008.

Burtless, Gary, and Christopher Jencks. 2003. "American Inequality and Its Consequences." *Agenda for the Nation*, edited by Henry J. Aaron, James M. Lindsay, and Pietro Nivola. Washington: The Brookings Institution.

Caplow, Theodore, Louis Hicks, and Ben J. Wattenberg. 2001. *The First Measured Century: An Illustrated Guide to Trends in America, 1900–2000.* Washington, D.C.: The American Enterprise Institute Press.

Carroll, Joseph. 2007. "Most Americans 'Very Satisfied' With Their Personal Lives." Gallup.

Centers for Disease Control and Prevention. 2009. "Summary of Notifiable Diseases—United States, 2007." *Morbidity and Mortality Weekly Report* 56(53).

Centers for Disease Control and Prevention. 2010. *HIV in the United States: An Overview.*

Central Intelligence Agency. 2010. *The CIA World Factbook 2010.* New York: Skyhorse Publishing.

Chen, Shaohua, and Martin Ravallion. 2008. "The Developing World Is Poorer than We Thought, But No Less Successful in Fighting Poverty." *World Bank Policy Research Working Paper* No. 4703.

Committee on Transportation and Infrastructure. 2008. *Stagnant Waters: The Legacy of the Bush Administration on the Clean Water Act.* Washington, D.C.

Coontz, Stephanie. 1992. *The Way We Never Were: American Families and the Nostalgia Trap.* New York: Basic Books.

Costa, Dora L. 2000. "The Wage and the Length of the Work Day: From the 1890s to 1991." *Journal of Labor Economics* 18(1): 156–181.

Council on Environmental Quality. 1980. *The Global 2000 Report to the President. Volume I: Entering the Twenty-First Century.* Washington, D.C.: Government Printing Office.

Cox, W. Michael, and Richard Alm. 1997. "Time Well Spent: The Declining *Real* Cost of Living in America." 1997 Annual Report, Federal Reserve Bank of Dallas.

Cox, W. Michael, and Richard Alm. 1999. *Myths of Rich & Poor: Why We're Better Off than We Think.* New York: Basic Books.

Crissey, Sarah R. 2009. "Educational Attainment in the United States: 2007." *Current Population Report* January, 2009. Washington: U.S. Census Bureau.

Deaton, Angus. 2008. "Income, Health, and Well-Being around the World: Evidence from the Gallup World Poll." *Journal of Economic Perspectives* 22(2).

DeNavas-Walt, Carmen, Bernadette D. Proctor, and Jessica C. Smith. 2008. *Insurance, Poverty, and Health Insurance Coverage in the United States.* Washington, D.C.: U.S. Census Bureau.

Donohue III, John J., and Steven D. Levitt. 2001. "The Impact of Legalized Abortion on Crime." *The Quarterly Journal of Economics* CXVI(2): 379–420.

Dye, Jane Lawler, and Tallese Johnson. 2009. "A Child's Day: 2006 (Selected Indicators of Child Well-Being)." *Current Population Reports* 70–118.

Easterbrook, Gregg. 2003. *The Progress Paradox: How Life Gets Better While People Feel Worse.* New York: Random House.

Easterlin, Richard A. 2000. "The Worldwide Standard of Living Since 1800." *The Journal of Economic Perspectives* 14(1): 7–26.

Economic Report of the President. 2010. *Economic Report of the President: Including the Annual Report of the Council of Economic Advisers.* Washington, D.C.: United States Government Printing Office.

Edwards, Brenda K. et al. 2009. "Annual Report to the Nation on the Status of Cancer, 1975–2006." *Cancer* 116: 544–573

Ehrlich, Paul R. 1968. *The Population Bomb.* New York: Sierra Club-Ballantine Books.

Ehrlich, Paul R. 1970. "Eco-Catastrophe!" Special Edition of *Ramparts* magazine.

Ehrlich, Paul R., and Anne H. Ehrlich. 1974. *The End of Affluence: A Blueprint for Your Future*. New York: Ballantine Books.

Elsom, Derek M. 1995. "Atmospheric Pollution Trends in the United Kingdom." *The State of Humanity*, 476–490, edited by Julian L. Simon. Oxford: Blackwell.

Environmental Protection Agency. 2000. *National Air Pollutant Emission Trends, 1900–1998*. Washington, D.C.: Triangle Park, NC: Office of Air Quality and Standards.

Environmental Protection Agency. 2010. Climate Change Indicators in the United States. Washington, D.C.: National Service Center for Environmental Publications.

Etzioni, Amita. 1993. "The State of the Art. Beyond the Alarmed vs. Satisfied Debate." *The Responsive Community* 4(1): 4–6.

European Institute for Crime Prevention and Control. 2010. International Statistics on Crime and Justice. Helsinki.

Fackelmann, Kathleen. 2008. "Drug Poisonings Deaths on the Rise." *USA Today* April 3, 2008.

Federal Interagency Forum on Child and Family Statistics. 2009. *America's Children: Key National Indicators of Well-Being, 2009*. Washington, D.C.: U.S. Government Printing Office.

Finer, Lawrence B. 2007. "Trends in Premarital Sex in the United States, 1954–2003." *Public Health Reports* 122: 73–78.

Finke, Roger, and Rodney Stark. 1992. *The Churching of America 1776–1990: Winners and Losers in Our Religious Economy*. New Brunswick, NJ: Rutgers University Press.

Fischer, Claude S., and Michael Hout. 2006. *Century of Difference: How America Changed in the Last One Hundred Years*. New York: Russell Sage Foundation.

Flynn, James R. 1987. "Massive IQ Gains in 14 Nations: What IQ Tests Really Measure." *Psychological Bulletin* 101(2): 171–191.

Food and Agriculture Organization of the United Nations. 2000. *The State of Food Insecurity in the World 2000*. Rome: FAO Publishing.

Food and Agriculture Organization of the United Nations. 2005. *Global Forest Resources Assessment 2005*. Rome: FAO Publishing.

Food and Agriculture Organization of the United Nations. 2009. *The State of Food Insecurity in the World 2009: Economic Crises–Impacts and Lessons Learned*. Rome: FAO Publishing.

Food and Agriculture Organization of the United Nations. 2010. *Global Forest Resources Assessment 2010*. Rome: FAO Publishing.

Foote, Christopher L., and Christopher F. Goetz. 2005. "Testing Economic Hypotheses with State-Level Data: A Comment on Donohue and Levitt." *Quarterly Journal of Economics* 123(1).

Freedom House. 2009. *Worst of the Worst: The World's Most Repressive Societies*. Washington, D.C.

Freedom House. 2010. *Freedom in the World*. 2010. Washington, D.C.

Gardner, Howard. 1983. *Frames of the Mind: The Theory of Multiple Intelligences*. New York: Basic Books.

Garner, C. Allen. 2006. "Should the Decline in Personal Saving Rate Be a Cause for Concern?" *Federal Reserve Bank of Kansas City Economic Review*, Second Quarter 2006.

Garte, Seymour. 2008. *Where We Stand: A Surprising Look at the Real State of Our Planet*. New York: AMACOM.

Gauthier, Anne H., Timothy M. Smeedeng, Frank F. Furstenberg Jr. 2004. "Are Parents Investing Less Time in Children? Trends in Selected Industrialized Countries." *Population and Development Review* 30(4): 647–671.

Geneva Declaration. 2008. *Global Burden of Armed Violence*. Geneva.

Gladwell, Malcolm. 2007. "None of the Above: What I.Q. Doesn't Tell You about Race." *The New Yorker*, December 17, 2007.

Glassner, Barry. 1999. *The Culture of Fear*. New York: Basic Books.

Gleick, Peter H., Meena Palaniappan, Mari Morikawa, and Jason Morrison. 2009. *The World's Water 2008–2009: The Biennial Report on Freshwater Resources*. Pacific Institute for Studies in Development, Environment, and Security. Washington D.C.: Island Press.

Goeller, H. E. 1995. "Trends in Nonrenewable Resources." *The State of Humanity*, chapter 31, edited by Julian L. Simon. Oxford: Blackwell.

Goklany, Indur M. 2002. "Much Ado about Warming." *Forum for Applied Research and Public Policy* 16(4): 40–46.

Goklany, Indur M. 2004. "Economic Growth, Technological Change, and Human Well-Being." *You Have to Admit It's Getting Better: From Economic Prosperity to Environmental Quality*, chapter 2, edited by Terry L. Anderson. Stanford, CA: Hoover Institution Press.

Goklany, Indur M. 2007. *The Improving State of the World: Why We're Living Longer,*

Healthier, More Comfortable Lives on a Cleaner Planet. Washington, D.C.: Cato Institute.

Goklany, Indur M. 2009a. "Is Climate Change the 'Defining Challenge of Our Age'?" *Energy & Environment* 20(3): 279–302.

Goklany, Indur M. 2009b. "Trapped Between the Falling Sky and the Rising Seas: The Imagined Terrors of the Impacts of Climate Change." Unpublished manuscript.

Goklany, Indur M. 2009c. "Deaths and Death Rates from Extreme Weather Events: 1900–2008." *Journal of American Physicians and Surgeons* 14(4): 102–109.

Goodin, Robert E., James Mahmud Rice, Michael Bittman, Peter Saunders. 2005. "The Time-Pressure Illusion: Discretionary Time vs. Free Time." *Social Indicators Research* 73(1): pp. 43–70.

Grantham, George W. 1995. "Agricultural Productivity before the Green Revolution." *The State of Humanity,* 364–375, edited by Julian L. Simon. Oxford: Blackwell.

Guttmacher Institute. 2009. *Facts on Induced Abortion Worldwide.* New York.

Guttmacher Institute. 2010. *Facts on Induced Abortion in the United States.* New York.

Guzman, Lina, Laura Lippman, Kristin Anderson Moore, and William O'Hare. 2003. "How Children Are Doing: The Mismatch between Public Perception and Statistical Reality." *Child Trends Research Brief,* 2003–2012.

Haines, Michael R. 1995. "Disease and Health through the Ages." *The State of Humanity,* 51–60, edited by Julian L. Simon. Oxford: Blackwell.

Hatcher, John. 1986. "Mortality in the Fifteenth Century: Some New Evidence." *The Economic History Review* 39(1): 19–38.

Hayward, Steven F., and Amy Kaleita. 2007. Index of Leading Environmental Indicators, Twelfth Edition. San Francisco: Pacific Research Institute.

Hayward, Steven F., 2008. Index of Leading Environmental Indicators, Thirteenth Edition. San Francisco: Pacific Research Institute.

Hayward, Steven F. 2009. Index of Leading Environmental Indicators, Fourteenth Edition. San Francisco: Pacific Research Institute.

Herper, Matthew, and Peter Kang. 2006. "The World's Ten Best-Selling Drugs." *Forbes* March 22, 2006.

Hoefert, Andreas, and Simone Hofer. 2006. *Prices and Earnings: A Comparison of Purchasing Power Around the Globe.* 2006 Edition. UBS AG, Wealth Management Research.

Hoff Sommers, Christina. 1995. *Who Stole Feminism? How Women Have Betrayed Women*. New York: Simon & Schuster.

Hollander, Jack. 2003. *The Real Environmental Crisis: Why Poverty, Not Affluence, Is the Environment's Number One Enemy*. Berkeley: University of California Press.

Hollingsworth, T. H. 1977. "Mortality in the British Peerage Families Since 1600." *Population* 32:323–352.

Holloway, Marguerite. 1999. "Flynn's Effect." *Scientific American*, January 13, 1999.

Hout, Michael, and Caroline Hanley. 2002. "The Overworked American Family: Trends and Nontrends in Working Hours, 1968–2001." "A Century of Difference" Working Paper, The Survey Research Center, University of California, Berkeley.

Human Security Report Project. 2009. *Human Security Report 2009/2010: The Causes of Peace and the Shrinking Costs of War*. Simon Fraser University, Canada.

Hunter, James Davison, and Carl Desportes Bowman. 1996. *The State of Disunion: 1996 Survey of American Political Culture*. Media Research Foundation.

Inglehart, Ronald F. 2008. "Changing Values among Western Publics from 1970 to 2006." *West European Politics* 31(1–2): 130–146.

Inglehart, Ronald, Roberto Foa, Christopher Peterson, and Christian Welzel. 2008. "Development, Freedom, and Rising Happiness: A Global Perspective (1981–2007)." *Perspectives on Psychological Science* 3(4): 264–285.

Jacobs, Jerry A., and Kathleen Gerson. 2001. "Overworked Individuals or Overworked Families? Explaining Trends in Work, Leisure, and Family Time." *Work and Occupations* 28(1): 40–63.

Joint United Nations Programme on HIV/AIDS. 2008. *Report on the Global HIV/AIDS Epidemic 2008*.

Jones, Jeffrey M. 2010. In U.S., Many Environmental Issues at 20-Year-Low Concern. Gallup, Inc.

Jones, Rachel K., Lawrence B. Finer, and Susheela Singh. 2010. *Characteristics of U.S. Abortion Patients, 2008*. New York: Guttmacher Institute.

Joyce, Ted. 2004. "Did Legalized Abortion Lower Crime?" *Journal of Human Resources* 39(1): 1–28.

Kahneman, Daniel, and Angus Deaton. 2010. "High Income Improves Evaluation of Life but Not Emotional Well-Being." *PNAS Early Edition*. www.pnas.org /cgi/doi/10.1073/pnas.1011492107

Kaplan, Robert D. 1994. "The Coming Anarchy." *Atlantic*, February 1994.

Keyssar, Alexander. 1995. "Trends in Unemployment in the United States." *The State of Humanity*, 196–207, edited by Julian L. Simon. Oxford: Blackwell.

Lacina, Bethany, and Nils Petter Gleditsch. 2005. "Monitoring Trends in Global Combat: A New Dataset of Battle Deaths." *European Journal of Population* 21:145–166.

Lane, Robert E. 2000. *The Loss of Happiness in Market Democracies*. New Haven: Yale University Press.

Lebergott, Stanley. 1995. "Long-Term Trends in the US Standard of Living." *The State of Humanity*, 149–160, edited by Julian L. Simon. Oxford: Blackwell.

Lemann, Nicholas. 2010. "School Work." *The New Yorker* September 27, 2010.

Levine, Robert, Suguru Sato, Tsukasa Hashimoto, and Jyoti Verma. 1995. "Love and Marriage in Eleven Cultures." *Journal of Cross-Cultural Psychology* 26(5): 554–571.

Lindgreen, Hugo. 2009. "Pessimism Porn: Soft Spot for Hard Times." *New York Magazine*, February 1, 2009.

Lomborg, Bjorn. 2001. *The Skeptical Environmentalist: Measuring the Real State of the World*. Cambridge: Cambridge University Press.

Lomborg, Bjorn. 2004. "The Skeptical Environmentalist." *You Have to Admit It's Getting Better: From Economic Prosperity to Environmental Quality*, chapter 1, edited by Terry L. Anderson. Stanford, CA: Hoover Institution Press.

Lomborg, Bjorn. 2008. "How to Get the Biggest Bang for 10 Billion Bucks." *Wall Street Journal*, July 28, 2008.

Maddison, Angus. 1995. *Monitoring the World Economy*. Paris: OECD Publishing.

Maddison, Angus. 1998. *Chinese Economic Performance in the Long-Run*. Paris: OECD Publishing.

Maddison, Angus. 2007. *The World Economy*. Paris: OECD Publishing.

McPherson, J. Miller, Lynn Smith-Lovin, and Matthew E. Brashears. 2006. "Social Isolation in America: Changes in Core Discussion Networks over Two Decades." *American Sociological Review* 71(3): 353–375.

Miringoff, Marc, and Marque-Luisa Miringoff. 1999. *The Social Health of the Nation: How America Is Really Doing*. New York: Oxford University Press.

Moore, Stephen, and Julian Simon. 2000. *It's Getting Better All the Time: 100 Greatest Trends of the Last 100 Years*. Washington, D.C.: Cato Institute.

Morris, Martina, and Bruce Western. 1999. "Inequality in Earnings at the Close of the Twentieth Century." *Annual Review of Sociology* 25: 623–657.

Mosher, William D., Anjani Chandra, and Jo Jones. 2005. "Sexual Behavior and

Selected Health Measures: Men and Women 15–44 Years of Age, United States, 2002." *Advance Data from Vital and Health Statistics;* no. 362. Hyattsville, MD: National Center for Health Statistics.

Murray, David, Joel Schwartz, and S. Robert Lichter. 2001. *It Ain't Necessarily So: How Media Make and Unmake the Scientific Picture of Reality.* Boston: Rowan & Littlefield Publishers.

Myers, David G. 2000. *The American Paradox: Spiritual Hunger in an Age of Plenty.* New Haven: Yale University Press.

National Cancer Institute. 2006. *SEER Cancer Statistics Review, 1975–2003.* Bethesda, MD.

National Center for Health Statistics. 2010. *Health, United States, 2009: With Special Feature on Medical Technology.* Hyattsville, MD.

National Marriage Project. 2009. *The State of Our Unions 2009: Marriage in America.* University of Virginia.

Nielsen Company. 2010a. *Three Screen Report.* Volume 8, First Quarter 2010. New York.

Nielsen Company. 2010b. *How People Watch: A Global Nielsen Consumer Report.* New York.

Oeppen, Jim, and James W. Vaupel. 2002. "Broken Limits to Life Expectancy." *Science* 296(10): 1030–1031.

Opdycke, Sandra, and Marque-Luisa Miringoff. 2008. *The Social Health of the States 2008.* Vassar College: Institute for Innovation in Social Policy.

Owen, David. 2004. "Why New York Is the Greenest City in America." *The New Yorker,* October 18, 2004.

Panagopoulos, Costas. 2006. "Obesity: The Polls-Trends." *Public Opinion Quarterly* 70(2): 249–268.

Pew Center on the States. 2008. *One in 100: Behind Bars in America 2008.* Washington, D.C.

Pew Forum on Religion and Public Life. 2008. *U.S. Religious Landscape: Religious Affiliation: Diverse and Dynamic.* Washington, D.C.: Pew Research Center. *www.pewforum.org.*

Pew Research Center. 2006a. *Looking Backward and Forward, Americans See Less Progress in Their Lives.* Washington, D.C.

Pew Research Center. 2006b. *Once Again the Future Ain't What It Used to Be.* Washington, D.C.

Pew Research Center. 2007. *Generation Gap in Values, Behaviors: As Marriage and Parenthood Drift Apart.* Washington, D.C.

Pew Research Center. 2008. *Inside the Middle Class: Bad Times Hit the Good Life.* Washington, D.C.

Pew Research Center. 2010. *Global Attitudes Project: A 22-Nation Pew Global Attitudes Survey.* Washington, D.C.

Pew Research Center for the People & the Press. 2009. *December 2009 Political Survey.* Washington, D.C.

Piketty, Thomas, and Emmanuel Saez. 2001. "Income Inequality in the United States, 1913–1998." *Working Paper #8467* of the National Bureau of Economic Research.

Plotnick, Robert, Eugene Smolensky, Eirik Evenhouse, and Siobhan Reilly. 2000. "The Twentieth Century Record of Inequality and Poverty in the United States." *The Cambridge Economic History of the United States, Volume 3*, 249–300, edited by Stanley Engerman and Robert Gallman. Cambridge: Cambridge University Press.

Preston, Samuel H. 1995. "Human Mortality throughout History and Prehistory." *The State of Humanity*, 30–36, edited by Julian L. Simon. Oxford: Blackwell.

Putnam, Robert D. 1997. "Foreword." John P. Robinson and Geoffrey Godbey, *Time for Life: The Surprising Ways Americans Use their Time*, xv–xviii. University Park, PA: The Pennsylvania State University Press.

Putnam, Robert D. 2000. *Bowling Alone.* New York: Simon & Schuster.

Rainforest Action Network. 2010. *Turning the Page on Rainforest Destruction.* San Francisco: Rainforest Action Network.

Rampey, B. D., G. S. Dion, and P. L. Donahue. 2009. *NAEP 2008 Trends in Academic Progress (NCES 2009–479).* National Center for Education.

Statistics, Institute of Education Sciences, U.S. Department of Education, Washington, D.C.

Rector, Robert. 1995. "How 'Poor' Are America's Poor?" *The State of Humanity*, 241–256, edited by Julian L. Simon. Oxford: Blackwell.

Reynolds, Alan. 2006. *Income and Wealth.* Santa Barbara, CA: Greenwood.

Rideout, Victoria J., Ulla G. Foehr, and Donald F. Roberts. 2010. *Generation M²: Media in the Lives of 8- to 18-Year-Olds.* Menlo Park, CA: Kaiser Family Foundation.

Ridley, Matt. 2010. *The Rational Optimist: How Prosperity Evolves.* New York: Harper.

Robinson, John, and Geoffrey Godbey. 2005. "Busyness as Usual." *Social Research* 72(2): 407–426.

Rossi, Peter H. 1987. "No Good Applied Social Research Goes Unpunished." *Society* 25(1): 73–79.

Saad, Lydia. 2007. "Perceptions of Crime Problem Remain Curiously Negative: More See Crime Worsening Rather than Improving." Princeton, NJ: Gallup.

Sabol, William J., Heather C. West, and Matthew Cooper. 2008. "Prisoners in 2008." *Bureau of Justice Statistics Bulletin*, December 2009, NCJ 228417. Washington, D.C.

Samuelson, Robert J. 1995. *The Good Life and Its Discontents: The American Dream in the Age of Entitlement, 1945-1995.* New York: Times Books.

Sayer, Liana C., Suzanne M. Bianchi, John P. Robinson. 2004. "Are Parents Investing Less in Children? Trends in Mothers' and Fathers' Time with Children." *American Journal of Sociology* 110(1): 1–43.

Schor, Juliet. 1999. "The New Politics of Consumption." *Boston Review*, Summer 1999.

Sedjo, Roger A., and Marion Clawson. 1995. "Global Forests Revisited." *The State of Humanity*, 328–345, edited by Julian L. Simon. Oxford: Blackwell.

Smock, Pamela J. 2000. "Cohabitation in the United States: An Appraisal of Research Themes, Findings, and Implications." *Annual Review of Sociology* 26: 1–20.

Sowell, Thomas. 2008. *Economic Facts and Fallacies.* New York: Basic Books.

Spierenburg, Pieter. 2008. *A History of Murder: Personal Violence in Europe from the Middle Ages to the Present.* Cambridge, UK: Polity.

Stone, Arthur, Joseph E. Schwartz, Joan E. Broderick, and Angus Deaton. 2010. "A Snapshot of the Age Distribution of Psychological Well-Being in the United States." *PNAS* 107(22): 9985–9990.

Stone, Daniel. 2009. "Selling the Silver Lining." *Newsweek* March 23, 2009.

Strow, Claudia W., and Brian K. Strow. 2006. "A history of divorce and remarriage in the United States." *Humanomics* 22(4): 239–257.

Tengs, Tammy O. et al. 1995. "Five-Hundred Life-Saving Interventions and Their Cost-Effectiveness." *Risk Analysis* 15(3): 369–390.

Thernstrom, Stephan, and Abigail Thernstrom. 1997. *America in Black and White: One Nation, Indivisible.* New York: Simon & Schuster.

Tiefenthaler, Jill. 2009. "SATs Do Not Take the Full Measure of a High School Student." *US News and World Report*, September 4, 2009.

UNESCO. 2007. *Education for All by 2015: Will We Make It?* Oxford: UNESCO Publishing/Oxford University Press.

United Nations. 2009. *Human Development Report 2009. Overcoming Barriers: Human Mobility and Development.* New York: United Nations Development Programme.

United Nations. 2010. *The Millennial Development Goals Report.* New York: United Nations.

United Nations Office on Drugs and Crime. 2009. World Drug Report 2009. Vienna.

U.S. Environmental Protection Agency. 2008. *Our Nation's Air: Status and Trends through 2008.* Washington, D.C.

United States Senate Committee on Environment and Public Works. 2006. *A Skeptic's Guide to Debunking Global Warming Alarmism.* Washington, D.C.: United States Senate.

Van Praag, Bernard M. S., and Paul Fijters. 1999. "The Measurement of Welfare and Well-Being." *Well-Being: The Foundations of Hedonic Psychology*, 413–433, edited by Daniel Kahneman, Ed Diener, and Norbert Schwarz. New York: Russell Sage Foundation Publications.

Veenhoven, Ruut, and Michael Hagerty. 2006. "Rising Happiness in Nations 1946–2004: A Reply to Easterlin." *Social Indicators Research* 79(3): 421–436.

Walmsley, Roy. 2008. World Prison Population List (Eighth Edition). London: International Centre for Prison Studies.

Want, Youfa, and Tim Lobstein. 2006. "Worldwide Trends in Childhood Overweight and Obesity." *International Journal of Pediatric Obesity* 1: 11–25.

Washington University in St. Louis. 1998. "Why Women Are Less Likely than Men to Commit Suicide." *ScienceDaily*, 12 November 1998.

Wattenberg, Ben J. 1984. *The Good News Is that the Bad News Is Wrong.* New York: Simon & Schuster.

Whaples, Robert. 2001. "Hours of Work in U.S. History." EH.Net Encyclopedia, edited by Robert Whaples. August 14, 2001. *http://eh.net/encyclopedia/article /whaples.work.hours.us* Accessed September 15, 2010.

Whitman, David. 1998. *The Optimism Gap: The I'm Ok—They're Not Syndrome and the Myth of American Decline.* New York: Walker and Company.

Wilcox, W. Bradford. 2009. "The Evolution of Divorce." *National Affairs,* Issue #1, Fall 2009.

Wilkinson, Richard G., and Kate E. Pickett. 2009. "Income Inequality and Social Dysfunction." *Annual Review of Sociology* 35:493–511.

World Almanac. 2010. *World Almanac and Book of Facts.* New York: World Almanac Books.

World Health Organization. 2002. *Self-Directed Violence.* Geneva.

World Health Organization. 2009. World Health Statistics 2009. Geneva: WHO Press.

Worldwatch Institute, The. 2009. *State of the World: Into a Warming World.* New York: W. W. Norton & Company.

Worldwatch Institute. 2003. *State of the World 2003.* Washington, D.C.

Xu, Jiaquan, Kenneth D. Kochanek, Sherry L. Murphy, and Betzaida Tejada-Vera. 2010. "Deaths: Final Data for 2007." *National Vital Statistics Reports* 58(19). Hyattsville, MD: National Center for Health Statistics.

Yandle, Bruce, Maya Vijayarghavan, and Madhusudan Bhattarai. 2004. "Income and the Race to the Top." *You Have to Admit It's Getting Better: From Economic Prosperity to Environmental Quality,* 83–108. Stanford: Hoover Institution Press.

ABOUT THE AUTHOR

Bradley Wright (PhD, University of Wisconsin) is Associate Professor of Sociology at the University of Connecticut, where he researches American Christianity. His first book, *Christians Are Hate-Filled Hypocrites . . . And Other Lies You've Been Told*, won the *Christianity Today* book award in the category of Christianity and Culture.

Brad blogs at *http://brewright.blogspot.com*. He is married, has two children, and lives in Storrs, Connecticut.